KNIT INK

(and Other Poems)

Deep Vellum Publishing
3000 Commerce Street, Dallas, Texas 75226
deepvellum.org · @deepvellum

Deep Vellum is a 501c3 nonprofit literary arts organization founded in 2013 with the mission
to bring the world into conversation through literature.

Originally published in the U.K. by Penteract Press as *Stray Arts (and Other Inventions)* (2019), *The Utu Sonnets* (2021), *Slate Petals (and Other Wordscapes)* (2021), and *The Noson Sonnets* (2022).

First U.S. edition, 2024

Support for this publication has been provided in part by grants from the National
Endowment for the Arts, the Texas Commission on the Arts, the City of Dallas Office of Arts
and Culture, the Communities Foundation of Texas, and the Addy Foundation.

Paperback ISBN: 9781646053452
Ebook ISBN: 9781646053469

LIBRARY OF CONGRESS CATALOGING-IN-PUBLICATION DATA:

Names: Etherin, Anthony, author. | Etherin, Anthony. Noson sonnets. 2022. |
Etherin, Anthony. Slate petals. 2021. | Etherin, Anthony. Stray arts.
2019. | Etherin, Anthony. Utu sonnets. 2021.
Title: Knit ink : (and other poems) / Anthony Etherin.
Other titles: Knit ink (Compilation)
Description: First US edition. | Dallas, Texas : Deep Vellum Publishing,
2024. | This work consists of two full-length collections, Slate petals
(and other wordscapes), Stray arts (and other inventions), and the
chapbooks The Noson sonnets and The Utu sonnets.
Identifiers: LCCN 2024001437 (print) | LCCN 2024001438 (ebook) | ISBN
9781646053452 (trade paperback) | ISBN 9781646053469 (ebook)
Subjects: LCGFT: Poetry.
Classification: LCC PR6105.T37 K55 2024 (print) | LCC PR6105.T37 (ebook)
| DDC 821/.92--dc23/eng/20240116
LC record available at https://lccn.loc.gov/2024001437
LC ebook record available at https://lccn.loc.gov/2024001438

Cover art and design by Anthony Etherin
Interior layout and typesetting by Anthony Etherin

PRINTED IN THE UNITED STATES OF AMERICA

KNIT INK

(and Other Poems)

ANTHONY ETHERIN

DEEP
VELLUM

DALLAS, TEXAS

Foreword

Anthony Etherin in *Knit Ink* has earned my most extreme plaudits, doing so by inducing in me a sense of envy—because, alas, he has written a book that I might have wished to have written myself. *Knit Ink* collects the best work by my peer, who (like me) has dedicated his career to the use of restrictive, formalistic constraints in the composition of poetry. Many of his works abide by a diverse variety of stern rules so rigorous that any form of meaningful expression under such duresses might seem, at first, impossible—and yet, despite such crippling embargoes, he nevertheless produces uncanny results, which seem to verge upon witchcraft. Many poets might have mastered the capacity to write two complementary sonnets according to the rules of the form, writing both in iambic pentameter: one Petrarchan in its rhyme scheme, one Shakespearean in its rhyme scheme. Few (if any) poets, however, might write two such poems in the way that Etherin does in his diptych "War Ends War." Both of his sonnets follow these traditional conventions—but not only is each poem also a palindrome (with a series of letters reading the same both forwards and reversed), both poems are also anagrams of each other (both sharing an identical inventory of letters, all rearranged). I know, from my own experience, that I might possess both the persistence and the wherewithal to accomplish such a feat myself, but only after untold months of labour (rather than the mere days of effort required by Etherin).

Knit Ink demonstrates this degree of prowess on each page, and yet most of these acrobatics might, otherwise, go unnoticed. The works often appear unlaboured and effortless (thereby enhancing the wonder of their accomplishment when the poet finally unveils their formal rigour at the end of the book). The poems, in fact, often feature motifs of pastoral, Romantic lyricism, taking their inspiration from the likes of John Keats (among others)—and thus we can appreciate these poems for the merits of their lyrical images and their musical tropes. These poems, however, invest themselves not in the expression of the self so much as in the sublimation of the self, subordinating the self to a rule in order to see what aesthetic potential the rule itself might unlock. The works indulge in an extreme version of what Keats might call "negative capability" (the capacity of the poet to "negate" themselves in order to make themselves receptive to "mysteries" that exceed the certitude of self-regard). We appreciate these poems, not because the self has provided evidence for its own authentic sincerity so much as we appreciate the degree to which the self can surprise itself, finding a means to evoke beauty even under conditions of exorbitant linguistic constraint. I admire these poems because they flirt with the "impossible"—and they testify to the fact that, despite any effort to curtail the power of language, to censor it with rules and dicta, language (like life itself) finds a way to thrive.

—Christian Bök

Introduction

Together here for the first time, the *Knit Ink* tetralogy consists of two full-length collections, *Slate Petals (and Other Wordscapes)* and *Stray Arts (and Other Inventions)*, and their respective chapbook epilogues, *The Noson Sonnets* and *The Utu Sonnets*.

This tetralogy explores the relationship between established poetic forms and alphabetical wordplay constraints (principally anagrams, palindromes, and their variants). In doing so, it embraces both tradition and experimentation, employing techniques both classical and avant-garde.

More specifically, *Knit Ink* explores the nature of poetry and meaning under various degrees of constraint. To this end, two complementary compositional approaches have been taken:

In the first, few constraints are employed simultaneously. The intention, under these circumstances, is to create poetry that foregrounds lyricism and meaning (to the extent that meaning is desirable). The goal is to achieve clarity of imagery and thought, in spite of alphabetical and metrical restriction.

In the second, multiple constraints are employed simultaneously. The intention here is to relinquish control over meaning, and to instead embrace the unusual music and slanted reality that literary restriction invites. The goal is to achieve an "alien voice" whose strangeness foregrounds the labyrinthine structure within which it was born.

The line between these two approaches is not always clear. However, while each book-chapbook pair follows both paths, it is evident that *Slate Petals* and *The Noson Sonnets* favour the first, while *Stray Arts* and *The Utu Sonnets* favour the second. Since the trajectory of each individual collection is towards increased constraint, I have chosen, in this edition, to present the books out of chronological order:

Slate Petals (and Other Wordscapes) (Penteract Press, 2021)
The Noson Sonnets (Penteract Press, 2022)
Stray Arts (and Other Inventions) (Penteract Press, 2019)
The Utu Sonnets (Penteract Press, 2021)

The books retain their original formatting and pagination, rather than being merged into a single design. This is to present the two book-chapbook pairs—and their favoured approaches to constraint (mentioned above)—as complementary opposites, thus emphasising *Knit Ink's* general theme of "*contraria sunt complementa*": In the universe of *Knit Ink*, tradition completes innovation, simplicity completes complexity, backwards completes forwards, and opacity completes clarity—sure as day completes night.

Throughout the books, textual poems are complemented by visual poetry—which I see as a natural companion to constraint: While constrained poetry explores the area between text and form, visual poetry explores that between text and image. While constrained poetry often deals in nonsemantic patterns of language, visual poetry often deals in nonsemantic patterns of writing—patterns formed from both alphabetical and nonalphabetical glyphs, and from both literary and non-literary lines.

Each of the books ends with further notes on the intentions of my poems, as well as details of the formal, alphabetical, and metrical restrictions underpinning them.

—Anthony Etherin

SLATE PETALS

(and Other Wordscapes)

ANTHONY ETHERIN

for Clara

Landscapes

THE DESERT   10

THE WONDER   11

TIME TURNS THE SHADOWS   12

COLOURSCAPE   13

LANDSCAPE   14

THE DALES   15

MOUNTAIN RANGE TRIOLET   16

THE HILLS   17

CROWSCAPES   18

BEES ON THE FERTILE HEATH   20

MATHEMATICS OF A FROZEN LAKE   21

WINTERSCAPES   22

WINTER SOLSTICE   23

THE WOODS ARE DEEP   24

LEAVES   25

CITY SCAFFOLD   26

CITYSCAPE   27

NAME THIS WORLD   28

Seascapes

MARINA   30

THE GULLS   31

ASEMIC TALES OF A COASTAL SLATE   32

WAVESCAPE   33

THE MAIN   34

THE SEA-SERPENT   36

ABOVE AND BELOW   37

THE ISLAND   38

Skyscapes

EARLY MOON   40

EARLY SUN   41

THE CLOUDS   42

THE SCATTERING   43

DOVE OF PIECES   44

THE DEPARTURE   45

NEAR SIDE OF THE MOON   46

FAR SIDE OF THE MOON   47

LUNAR PHASES SESTINA   48

MOON IN A WATERFALL   49

YOUR STAR   50

I LOVE THE STARS   51

THE COMET, AT MIDNIGHT   52

THE SMALLEST STARS   53

NOIR OF ORION   54

THE LITERATURE OF STARS   55

PALIMPSEST   56

Mindscapes

JULY   58

SOLEMN   59

TRIONNET   60

VERSESCAPES   62

A VILLANELLE   64

LOVE SONNET OF THE CAUTIOUS ROMANTIC   65

NEW INK   66

KNIT INK   67

THIS STATUS IS JOY   68

THE RAVEN   69

LAMENTS OF A CARVED WOODEN OWL   70

DREAMS OF A PAPER SWAN   71

WANTS OF AN AGEING DOLL   72

THOUGHTS OF A HUMAN ADRIFT   73

THE ALCHEMIST   74

AN INCANTATION   75

OF MUSIC AND MEMORY   76

MARIONETTE NOIR A.M.   78

THEATRESCAPES   79

DRINKS FOR DIONYSUS   80

OF WINE AND WORDS   81

FREE WILL (IT'S ALL NEURONS)   82

FLAVOURS   83

WAVEFUNCTIONS (IT'S ALL OBSERVATION)   84

Lorescapes

THE TOWER   86

EVER AFTER   87

BEAUTY   88

SPINNING GOLD   90

THE BANSHEE   92

THE VAMPIRE   93

KELPIES   94

THE WILD HUNT   95

PHANTOMS   96

THE DEVIL   97

THE GREEN CHILDREN OF WOOLPIT   98

GODIVA   99

AVALON   100

OTHERWORLD   102

Endscapes

DEATHSCAPE 104

DEATH OF THE SUN, MOON, AND STARS 105

THE COFFIN 106

OBLIVION 107

END TIMES 108

I LEAVE TORN 110

THE UNDERTAKER 111

RUNICALLY UNLYRICAL 112

RAGNARÖK 113

CHAOS AND RESURRECTION 114

OMEGAS 116

ALPHA AND OMEGA 117

WAR ENDS WAR 118

Formscapes

LANDSCAPES 123

SEASCAPES 127

SKYSCAPES 128

MINDSCAPES 130

LORESCAPES 134

ENDSCAPES 136

CONCISION AND CONSTRAINT 139

REGARDING THE AELINDROME 143

PRAISE FOR SLATE PETALS 146

PREVIOUS PUBLICATIONS 147

LANDSCAPES

The Desert

Char asserts Eden,
a desert sea's arch....

Moody, burned dust....
Oh, still aerify!

My ravine defoliated,
dim, its mirage bit.

Sure no bliss of pools to order,
still its red roots loop fossil bone.

Rust,
I beg a rim's
timid detail of Eden.

I vary my fire:
All its hot, sudden, ruby doom.

The Wonder

Wonder erases
or passes, someway, my awe.
Mosses, sap....
Roses are red now.

More winter seedlings —
more needless writing;
entire worlds seeming
to merge in wilderness....

I write legend's sermon,
melting roses' red wine.
I twirl green, Eden moss.
I grow tenderness lime.
Now mingled, trees rise —
emerge, silent in words.

Lore sings! Wed in metre,
one wilder stem reigns —
its lime green wonders
resting on red. We smile
in Eden's grim, low trees —
omen wrestling desire.

Time engineers worlds....

Time Turns the Shadows

Sun up, still....
A sun I saw.

Time grew old.

A sad,
lower gem,
it was in us all.

It spun us.   Sun us!

                     I emit wards —
                     gel still, a wan opus
                     upon a wall....

                     Its legs
                     draw time.

                     I sun us.

Time keeps forever.   It grows us in light.
    The unfurling days see shadows turn.
In turn,   shadows see days unfurling.
The light in us grows.   It forever keeps time.

Colourscape

Nature painted this morning
as a thorn in untried pigment,
a mad night in turpentines, or
the turning points in a dream....

The night
was green.
It might
A day that might have been was painted black.
A brush erased the moss and amber leaves.
Then, any light that came was given back —
consumed and flung across aborted eves —
as time and space, the frame, began to crack....
Beneath the new, the old dimension grieves:
That day became stained glass — an onyx mass.
Soon, every truth I'm told will likewise pass.
the grass
and dew
were blue.

Landscape

An endless pale,
dense alps encase
a deepened dale —
a deeded place:
A leaden sand
leased seeded leas;
a sleepless land
cascades appease.

Canals as clean
as essence pass
a ceaseless scene
and dance.... (Alas,
an apple seed
pens Eden's deed....)

The Dales

Melody, abloom,
treads a dale
in gloomy March.
    A season,
    and he abandons
    a search.
        May,
        looming,
        leads a dream
        to a bloody elm....

We save
long-lost mounts,
and I rain,
led again in shades,
the river thus a dream....
    Rest up. Go upstream.
        Read us the river:
        the sad shining —
            a dale, in radiant sun;
            most long loves' awe....

Mountain Range Triolet

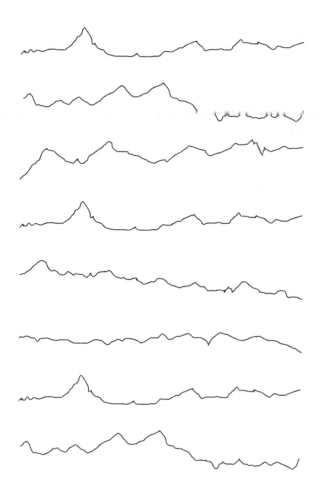

The Hills

A mar on a past, idle hill....
It's a still I held.
It's a panorama.

There, the hills speak inwards.
Spirits walk, harden the heels,
while sharper, naked thistles

skewer shins. The pallid earth
enthrals — like Death's whisper.

We listen.... The dark has her lips,
this skeletal wind her phrase....

Crowscapes

CROW ABOVE

Deft,
I saw a crow,
over us,
a sure vow or caw
as it fed.

MURDER OF CROWS

A murder, from a garden, rose
and left us in the dying light.
The sky is red now — no one knows
a murder from a garden rose.
It's rare to see so many crows,
and now they've gone to gather night.
A murder from a garden rose
and left us in the dying light.

THE CREEK

The crows are back at the
weathercock that bears
a hawk.... Both trace secret
arches to the backwater,
to caw at the brash creek....

THE CHURCH

They stop
and perch
atop
the church,
a choir
below
the spire:
The crows.
Each caw
enlists
ten more.
The mist
is grey
as clay.

Bees on the Fertile Heath

You hone yields
and inform us.
You perform in fields
and you honey....

Slate pots
    met speedy
        bees, I see,
            by deep stems,
                to petals....

                The bees have left their lonely
                hive. They float, serene. (The bell
                tolls here — the feeble, heavy tin....)
                They flee, over beaten hills (the
                level ones, by the fertile heath).
                They are fell, the noble thieves —
                rebel lives that flee the honey.

Mathematics of a Frozen Lake

Slam ice, dynamic.
A bad loch: Cold abaci.
Many decimals....

Rested ice
pools cold flakes
now
on a winter's lake.

I cement a thematic oasis;
see main abaci,
all glacial,
in a basis —
see mathematic omen take.

Ice inters law.

Snow, on a lake!
Fold ice,
pools crested....

Winterscapes

WINTER WAILS

Winter wails lavish frost:
Snowfall arrives, with its
faint silver. (Slow wraiths
flow in salt rivers.) What is
final swirls over its thaw.

WINTER MISTS

We noted a froth —
gilded, iced too....
Mists or fleets
dip mildness.
Won, snows send
limpid, steel frosts.
I moot decided light —
or fade to new.

WINTER SINKS

Winter sinks through its lonely
silk, to hungrily rest in the snow.
(It turns in the sky.) One girl howls
your ghost — winter's knell, in this
thornless, white inking.... So truly
the girl knows its ruin. Honestly:
try on its white skull, on her sign.

Winter Solstice

Winter Solstice:
Nights echo wide
in the cosmic web.
Time confides....
In her low light, we
find the old rites.

    Winter Solstice:
    Written close is
    woe. Strict lines
    wrestle in stoic
    selections, writ
    low in its secret....

        Winter Solstice:
        Concentric stones
        enclose its stillness.
        Soon, esoteric
        silence rises
        in its lit concerto.

            Winter Solstice:
            Silver shimmers
            needle darkness.
            Gilded lanterns
            gently splinter
            leaden mornings....

The Woods Are Deep
(or, The Knotted Tree)

Leaves

Late plan. Mutual.
La fête d'été.
Fall, autumnal petal....

Whose sorrow grew these hanging hosts
that rustle in the endless breeze?

The forest holds a court of ghosts
whose sorrow grew. (These hanging hosts

were sentinels of ancient posts,
but now are noosed to nameless trees.)

Whose sorrow grew these hanging hosts?
That rustle, in the endless breeze....

City Scaffold

The neon is exact.	T————————————T
It holds variety:	—T——————————T—
A stony, old hotel.	——T————————T——
Elite societies.	————T——————T————
A unity, in stereo	T——————T————
and city stimuli.	——————T——T—————
(A vacant tenancy,	——————TT————
in quiet tyranny.	——————TT————
A mighty stadium.	——————T——T—————
A vintage studio....)	—————T—————T—————
One tenement am I;	———T————————T———
in time, a capital:	——T——————————T——
A tally of events —	—T————————————T—
to occupy cement....	T——————————————T

Cityscape

Go flat, urbanised....
A cradle here held arcades
in a brutal fog.

That city grew
from many reds —
each busy view
from clay that bled;
each rosy lamp
from iron rust;
each cosy camp
from ruby dust.

Fate dyed your town:
When wind blew hard,
pink mist fell down
upon your yard
like arid rain —
hued deep with pain.

Name This World

(or, The Failed Cartographer)

Demand a hill,
at solid nadir....
      Damn it!
      One morn,
      I saw I was
      in Rome,
      not in Madrid,
      and I lost all I had named....

          Letters meddled.
             Now,
             Rome is a *Rima*.
             London
             is London
             no more.
                Deeds hide,
                and I'm alone
                in the model town....

SEASCAPES

Marina

A dock.
Sudden ways,
tides....
I arose,
so raised
its yawned, dusk coda.

Hear that solemn rain
on the marina: Her salt

aroma. The snarl in the
lather.... This near moan

alarms another, in the
harsher lamentation....

The Gulls

Go, feel
freed. All abyss, algae   saw
a sloop, one vocal lugsail. As you based it
on wash,   surf, or a wade, I died.
A war of rush saw no tides....
A buoy's alias: *Gull.* A cove
(no pool)   saw a sea.
Glassy   balladeer,
flee   fog....

By light,
we mull
their lull
of flight
and white
of skull —
but gulls,
tonight,
will flock
to shore
and swarm
the dock
before
the storm....

Asemic Tales of a Coastal Slate

Wavescape

The seas, with crests
and clouds of white,
have vowed unrest
to me, at night.
They'll flee — the waves
so loud awake,
unbowed in caves,
and free to break —
then spill their bones,
like ink on glyphs
or ghosts of stone,
to fill the cliffs,
and sink beside
the coasts, the tide....

The seas
and clouds
have vowed
to me
they'll flee —
so loud,
unbowed,
and free —
then spill
like ink
or ghosts,
to fill
and sink
the coasts....

With crests
of white
unrest,
at night,
the waves
awake
in caves,
to break
their bones
on glyphs
of stone:
the cliffs
beside
the tide.

The Main

RISEN SIREN	POISONED POSEIDON
In opal day,	Poseidon spilt
a siren swarm,	Aegean Sea.
a gauge away,	A league rebuilt
allowed a form.	your wail of plea.
I aged. (I look	Yet, oil amid
a trident's leap;	a plying dark,
your open book	a nereid
in idle deeps....)	flew up a spark:
One ripple woke.	"Poseidon, look!
I sailed up brine.	A godly sign."
Atop, God spoke	A drowned god took
a pious line:	a poison-wine.
"To Glory! — Land	Poseidon bled
of gilded sand!"	a primal red.

MAN-O-WAR

Keels, in a tide,
keep rid and log.
I buoy, topside
pooled under fog....

I ran. I saw
pools yell a gap:
a man-o'-war,
raw, on a map.

A galley-sloop
was in a rig
of red: Nude, looped,

I spot you! Big
old nadir peeked,
I tan, I *sleek*....

SLOOP-O-WAR

On lookout, see
a sloop-of-war,
its sodden floor
askew to me....

I dipped: "Pray, we!"
(A siren's roar!
In pagan lore,
I keep a key.)

A gale, by gull;
a winding main;
a saline odd

obeyed a lull,
applied our pain.
God pitied God.

The Sea-Serpent

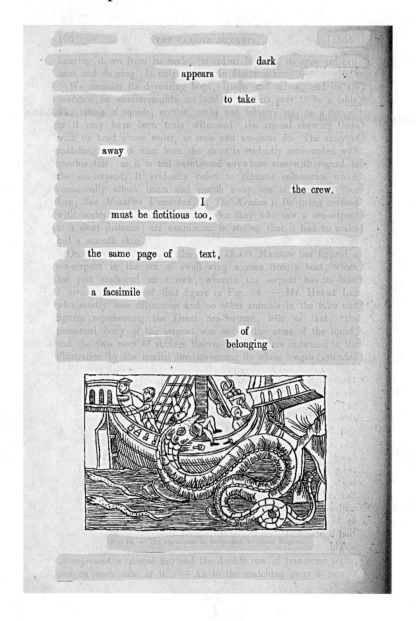

hanging down from its neck, its colour is **dark**, its eyes are brilliant and flaming. It only **appears** in fine weather.

We consider its devouring hogs, lambs and calves, and its appearance on summernights on land **to take** its prey to be a fable. Its chewing rorquids, cuttles, crabs and lobsters, or it may have been truly witnessed, the animal chewing them with its head above water, as seals and sea-lions do. The story of snatching **away** a man from the ships is evidently confounded with another tale, as it is not mentioned anywhere else with regard to the sea-serpent. It evidently refers to gigantic calamaries which occasionally attack boats and snatch away one of **the crew.** (See Lee, *Sea Monsters Unmasked, The Kraken*.) Its being covered with scales **I must be fictitious too,** for they who saw a sea-serpent at a short distance, are unanimous in stating that it had no scales but a smooth skin.

On **the same page of** the **text,** Olaus Magnus has figured a sea-serpent in the act of swallowing a man from a boat, which has just anchored on a rock, wherein the serpent has its hole. I give **a facsimile** of that figure in Fig. 14. — Mr. Henry Lee who mostly sees calamaries and no other animals in the tales and figures representing the Great Sea-Serpent, tells us that, "the presumed body of the serpent was one **of** the arms of the squid, and the two rows of suckers thereto **belonging** are indicated in the illustration by the medial line traversing its whole length (intended

Fig. 14. — The sea-serpent as represented by Olaus Magnus.

to represent a dorsal fin) and the double row of transverse septa, one on each side of it". — As to the snatching away a man of

36

Above and Below

Desire stowed ships on seas,
while air, a fragrant eddy, ran....
A fragile air whips on.
Seas wed shores, tides....

For every wave that swallows ships,
there's one that spits them from the sea.

(Abyssal serpents lick their lips,
for every wave that swallows ships.)

For every mast the seas eclipse,
you'll find another rising free.

(For every wave that swallows ships,
there's one that spits them from the sea....)

The Island

Raft ropes, nets,
you befilth cay isles.
Seven old, lone vessels....
I yacht —
lifebuoys tense, port far.

The river dries
by summer's heat.
The island ties.
Its people meet.

Then, water carves
its autumn smile
and, once more, halves
the knitted isle,

till none recall
who lives across
the river's wall.

The sense of loss
itself is lost
by winter's frost.

SKYSCAPES

Early Moon

Early, misty Moon.
My solitary omen.
My rain looms, yet
it's only a memory....

I'm my story alone:
Timely moonrays
lit my years.... Moon,
my many roots lie
in a mystery — loom
on, or lay my times....

Early, misty Moon:
my solitary omen.
It's only a memory.
(It's only a memory.)

Early Sun

Early morning Sun.
My angels' iron urn.
Mean glory runs in
many longer ruins.

Luna, in merry song,
moans unerringly —
a sly, morning rune,
slurring any omen;
luring any sermon
my inner soul rang.

Early morning Sun.
My angels' iron urn.
Many longer ruins.
(Many longer ruins.)

The Clouds

Sky white. Rain,
as fawns adorn my morns....
A dawn
as fainter whisky.

The clouds don't know what shape to be;
that's why two never look the same.

That's why they drift. For all they see,
the clouds don't know what shape to be.

They form and spill; they fade and flee,
oblivious of nature's aim.

The clouds don't know what shape to be —
that's why two never look the same.

The Scattering

The sun is white and nuclear
but comes to us as yellow fire.
(Indifference, scattered, brings desire.)
The sun is white. The sun is white.

The white of the sky is deflected to blueness,
refracted to rainbows, and shifted to shimmers —
a colourful congress of glistening glimmers.
The white of the sky is the white of the sky is...

There is fear when it is cloudy that the scattering is over,
since the clouds affect a lightness that is tantamount to whiteness,
and our atmosphere appears to be consumed by solar brightness.
There is fear when it is cloudy. There is fear when it is cloudy.

Dove of Pieces

For Jove
above
(and love),
it wove
and dove,
this dove,
its glove
a cove,
a groove
or grove,
to move
and rove —
to prove
it strove....

The Departure

Removed, I demand
with wings I soar.
So, sing with wind....
Made, dive more.

The birds
had gone.
We heard
No clouds, not one. July was still as stone.
The sky could find no call upon its breath.
The sun was glass. All month, it ruled alone.
No clouds. Not one. July was still as stone.
When August came, the air would pass a groan:
the ache of time — and all its love and death.
No clouds, not one: July was still — as stone,
the sky could find no call upon its breath.
or quill
to scare
the air....

Near Side of the Moon

A loneliness finds images....
Selene is a land of missing
seas — and long, fine similes.

The Moon,
despite
its white
lagoon,
has strewn
tonight
blue light,
maroon
by dawn
and lost
to sun —
withdrawn,
like frost
unspun.

Far Side of the Moon

Wonder:
a dark side;
to me, rarer....
A remote disk —
radared now.

Far side of the Moon:
A stricken bone blooms
a hidden ode of rock.

Facing the open cosmos,
that silent stone looms —

a view for the long lost....

Lunar Phases Sestina

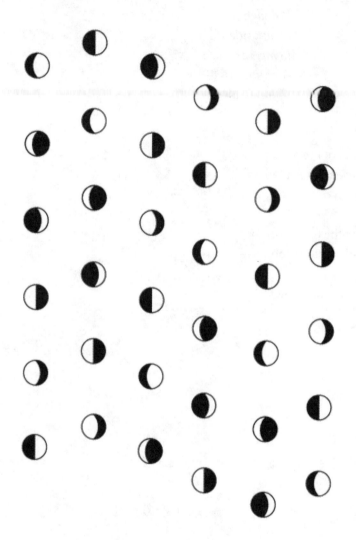

Moon in a Waterfall

Light blue
streams slowly fall.
 The moonshine —
 into water — spills night.
 The above is below.
 The below is above.
 The night spills
 water into moonshine.
 The fall slowly
 streams blue light....

 A null lore, now:
 One lost,
 solo slab,
 benign
 in a waxing of pity....
 A rapid,
 I dip a ray,
 tip fog —
 nix a waning,
 in ebb, also —
 lost,
 sole,
 now one,
 roll
 Luna....

Your Star

Deep suns obey
each fall, each rise.
Dusk dips away
like idle eyes....

When days were kind,
time made this plan.
Let's duly mind
when once you'd scan

that dark afar
with care: You'd name,
till dawn, each star....

Come! Play that game!
We'll find them fast:
Your star. Your past.

I Love the Stars

I love the stars, but most don't mean
that much to me. Most names elude
me. Some apparent magnitudes
are so faint that they can't be seen
by eye or, even, by machine.
Most azimuths and altitudes
are too aloof to be reviewed,
and stellar spectra often lean
toward the lean. But, helplessly,
I love the stars, as stars love night —
which is, of course, to say that they
too love that which they cannot see,
since astral bodies forge the light
and know but one unbroken day....

The Comet, at Midnight

At midnight, as I watch the scattered sky
and contemplate a trillion other earths,
a single, vivid comet passes by —
its brittle glitter breaking from the dearth....

The void is never void, nor still the night —
and fullness is so desolate and stark.
At midnight, as I gather all the light
inside myself, I gather all the dark....

Profusion is but paucity's repose:
Composers know that multitudes reside
inside the vacant stave. The sculptor knows
embodiment is formlessness untied....

And, falling from this canvas painted black,
the comet is a splinter of its lack.

The Smallest Stars

The smallest stars can fit inside a coffee mug.
(But few attempt it.) Tiny stars devour the rays
they radiate. They warp the rest. They pull and tug.
They strain and stress. They hide inside a blackened blaze....

The smallest stars can nestle in a miner's lamp,
but fall much darker than the cavern's dampest ditch —
their centres pulled along an asymptotic ramp,
a deft ascent to timeless time and pitchless pitch.

The smallest stars infest the night, but never shine
(their matter has no love for constellated arts);
instead, they gravely play a game of dark design
and stand unseen between the figures light imparts.

The *smallest* star, of course, is All: Completely curled.
Eternally unfurled. The first and final world....

Noir of Orion

The Literature of Stars

The Moon becomes a question mark, with Mars
below its waxing crescent arc, tonight.
Let's contemplate the literature of stars:

Andromeda is penning dark grimoires
(her spells are full of heat, but barely bright) —
the Moon becomes a question mark with Mars.

Now, Libra's writing enigmatic noirs,
while Leo crafts a parody with bite.
Let's contemplate the literature of stars.

The upper blackness hides Orion's scars,
yet buckles beam with tales of gallant might.
The Moon becomes a question mark, with mars.

Although they speak a language far from ours,
and many write their words in buried light,
let's contemplate the literature of stars.

Because their astral epic often jars
with all those ancient legends we recite,
the Moon becomes a question mark with Mars....
Let's contemplate the literature of stars.

Palimpsest

The night sky is a palimpsest
of stars: The living suns. The dead.
The distant and the near. They thread
their rays through space and time, compressed
and stretched. Their shifting infrared
is painted like a rose — undressed,
among the constellations blessed
with light. They tremble overhead.

They sink inside the morning sky —
a palimpsest obscured below
a palimpsest — before the clouds
emerge to write their own reply....
I wonder what initial glow —
what text — invoked these layered shrouds...?

MINDSCAPES

July

I walked a starlit field that cold July.
I found a star and named it after you,
the way the ancients mapped the gods to sky.

I named another for myself and drew
a line between us. Then, I said goodbye....

I wonder if the stars have named us too,
with names that last far longer than our own —
and echo, gently, mid that great unknown?

Solemn

I sat, solemn.
I saw time open one poem.
It was in me, lost as I.

In an ode,
I am lines of echoed woe,
blind as lines of air.

A set soul moans
awe, to map a neon poem
to woe's name — alas, it's I.

Trionnet

I've never been a soul content to live with fixed restraint.
Of course, despite that plea, I might invent my own and see
the vital force of freedom through that old complaint: constraint.

I've never been a soul content. To live with fixed restraint
might be the answer! So, I'll stroll the maze, escape to paint
a scene determined by restrictions mixed by none but me!

I've never been a soul content to live with fixed restraint.
Of course, despite that plea, I might invent my own and see....

SONNET

I've never been a soul content
to live with fixed restraint. Of course,
despite that plea, I might invent
my own and see the vital force
of freedom through that old complaint:
constraint. I've never been a soul
content. To live with fixed restraint
might be the answer! So, I'll stroll
the maze, escape to paint a scene
determined by restrictions mixed
by none but me! I've never been
a soul content to live with fixed
restraint. Of course, despite that plea,
I might invent my own and see....

Versescapes

TWENTY LETTERS, TEN LINES

In these twenty letters,
we try ten lines. The test
set, we tether sly intent.
We net the stint tersely.
We intently test ethers.
We try the silent tenets —
try the new, tense titles.
Written, the steely nest
therein settles twenty.
We enter its tenth style.

A SONNET

As seasons tease
a toast anon,
so neatness sees
a set as one.
Sonatas soon
atone, to sate
a neon noon.
Notes assonate.
A neat sestet
attests to stone —
a sonant net,
a tenet's tone —
as assets test
a sonnet's nest.

RIME, IN CONSTRAINT

Met I
a sonnet's rime,
in a lent pastoral,
or a poem
atemporal —
or a toast,
penal
in merits,
neon
as time....

ACROSTIC

Around
Constraint,
Resound
Or paint
Some thought
To stroll
In taut
Control....
See lines
Obey
New signs
Now they
Explore
Their law.

A Villanelle

Motifs compel
me now to free
a villanelle.

Restrictions sell
the melody
motifs compel.

Allusions swell
in harmony —
a villanelle

whose echoes yell
the formulae
motifs compel.

A sacred spell.
A symphony.
A villanelle.

I hear it tell
its form to me:
motifs compel
a villanelle....

Love Sonnet of the Cautious Romantic

If I could bring the Moon to you,
I wouldn't. No; it's needed where
it is. If I could walk us through
the corridors of time and share
a kiss with you in ancient rains,
afloat on some Edenic lake,
I think that, given causal chains,
the trip would be a big mistake.
If I could gather every rose
and from their petals weave a bed,
I'd feel the ecosystem's woes
upon me, and I'd count the dead....
       But poems are, my love, inert.
       I'll give you this — this cannot hurt.

New Ink

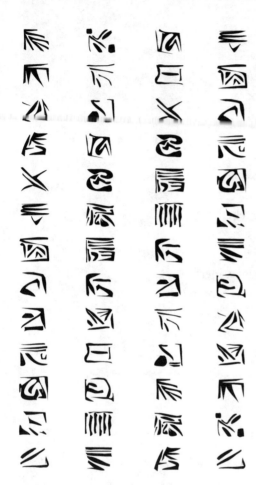

Knit Ink

Spill a poem:
its selfless sensuousness,
selfless time,
opal lips....

Words come to us like particles
of age; each prefix, stem, and root;
we thumb and tongue the articles,
each page of history's verbal loot,
and think of how the terms permute
about a visual pivot named
the ink — and how it's never tamed.
We speak without a sound
but with a shape, and send
the page our voice unbound.
No speech escapes. It's penned
to time. By choice, we blend
the ink; we fill the pot;
we hold the quill.... *We jot.*

This Status is Joy

I have confused
the letters
that were in
the poem

and which
you were busily
scribbling
for a book

Forgive me
they were a pale view
so sad
and so exact

The Raven

Shadows in the lamp-light beating,
    all the ghosts within repeating,
doubting, dreaming rare and radiant books of ancient lore...
    then, as though to name my sorrow,
    faintly, gently you came rapping,
and so aptly you came tapping, tapping at my chamber door.
Let my words be nothing, maiden ever rapping at my soul,
    but my darkness evermore.

Marvelled, I had flung the fancy,
    when the chamber murmured ghastly,
and in stepped a stately fowl of melancholy black.
    Caught by some ungainly flutter,
    stronger, now, I sought to utter —
till I more than merely muttered distant burdens back
to the silence of the chamber and the bird above my door.
    And we both said, "Nevermore!"

Fiery angel, never flitting,
    still there sitting, still there sitting,
sculptured eyes now ever at my pallid chamber door....
    Demon of the sainted maiden,
    horrors bleak in whispered dreaming,
dreary embers of thy shadow clasp my lonely soul
in the feathers of a raven. And my form, from out that midnight,
    shall be lifted nevermore.

Laments of a Carved Wooden Owl

> *Too honed, am I not?*
> *I sleep, I do.*
> *Owl as a basal wood.*
> *I peel, sit on....*
> *I made no hoot.*

A bitter scowl
upon its beak —
an inner shriek,
a buried howl —
this wooden owl,
its will is weak;
it cannot speak
a single vowel.
It makes no hoot
and draws no air,
so moot and mute;
its feathers bare,
its pain acute —
to wit, despair.

Dreams of a Paper Swan

Met,
I am read in answer —
a paper swan,
in a dreamtime....

Dawning's paper swan:
Thistles flow. Her body lies,
unlocking a dream....

    Midday's paper swan:
    Folding in her skin, to grace
    walls below the sun.

Nighttime's paper swan:
Snow falls idly on her back —
a deluge in words.

    Winter's paper swan:
    Resting by a mindful lake —
    holding shadow close.

Wants of an Ageing Doll

We fade — if sit aside —
yet eyes are senile; gait is ill.
O, dates pull, upset a doll.
I sit... I age...
lines erase,
yet, eyed, I satisfied a few....

The doll has cast its eye on you;
it tries a thousand smiles.... (That die —
the one you held but never threw —
the doll has cast.) Its eye on you,
it wants to crawl beside you, too.
It wishes you could hear it cry.
The doll has cast its eye on you;
it tries a thousand smiles that die.

Thoughts of a Human Adrift

Can we suppose man created God?
There is nothing suggesting we are divine.
Are we suggesting nothing is there?
"God created man" — suppose we can?

We don't belong — yet here we are,
adrift atop a cloud so rare
and wonderful it's flown too far.
We don't belong yet, here: We are
the only beast that maps the stars —
we're reaching for a kingdom where
we don't belong yet. Here we are,
adrift atop a cloud so rare....

The Alchemist

There's magic in blood:
A sober, demonic light
directs haemoglobin —
This iron became gold.

OUR SPELL ECHOES NOTED
MAGIC. APT ORE BREATHES
FROM THE MASON'S BLOOD.

Allot	Create
Ashen	Gold
Ether:	From
Dipped	A
Ferrous	Commensurate
Cogs	Base;
Become	Blood,
Another	The
Atom	Philosophers'
Blossom.	Stone.

An Incantation

Drawn in me,
lost,
some rite rises:
reverb,
most
solemnised ode....

It is all
as I tied.

Odes,
in me,
lost sombre verses.

I retire,
most solemn,
inward.

Raw, mid nests,
I'm mine.

Morose lord,
I bless ever a desire.

Soon,
test lit tilt.
Set noose.

Rise....

Dare, vessel,
bid roles or omen.

I'm mist's end.
I'm war.

Red root,
time ill,
I memos stir....
We mass, send nil....

Bones reverse.

Do it — as,
sat,
I odes reverse.

No blindness,
same writs.

Some mill,
I emit,
to order.

Of Music and Memory

<u>DISTANT MUSIC</u>

Emote to me. Refill a note.
By eking, I sedate my awe.

Now all I give, lines dash, promote,
to visit inward — rose, yet raw.

Art eyes, or drawn it is. I vote
to morph sad, senile vigil.... Law,

one way, met a design I key.
Be tonal, life remote to me!

DISTANT MEMORY

I grow a distant memory
of yellow petals knit in verse.

I weave the woodland's eye, to see —
I grow a distant memory.

I bleed time gone. I leave, to be
a limitation I rehearse:

I grow, a distant memory
of yellow — petals, knit in verse.

Marionette Noir a.m.

Theatrescapes

HEAD IN

See a play I'm in.
Adhere!
A theatre!
A theatre! — Head in.
I may please....

EMPTY THEATRE

At the empty theatre, I was busy drinking
whiskey by the pint. I made a stranger tut.
He turned away, striking this empty beat —
but I kept rhythm. I was in a tense tragedy,
rethinking ideas better put away; myths
that weary my sun.... I'd kept the rising beat,
by angry muster, and I kept its white heat,
but the needy spirit was taking my heart....

THESPIANS

These thespians soothed
the gathering. They breathed — then
the theatre breathed.

Drinks for Dionysus

> In the dark, we praise Dionysus,
> and deep in whiskey is our star....
> "His drunken awe is poetry," said
> the disarray kissed upon wine....
> "You raise the drinks, and we sip."

Set astray, men, I wade....

Resorb benightedness,
murmur lager.
(No daisy, no idyll. A unit....)

No cognacs
can go continually.

Dionysia,
don regal rum!

Rums sendeth gin,
ebb rosé, red —
a wine my art sates.

Of Wine and Words

The vine upstream is long,
inspires my ink — I play
this lyre in dreams or songs
of mine — We drink today
its wine and sink below
a pyre of grace, a world
whose fires rethink, bestow,
align and trace, unfurled
in graft, the space that burns
to light all words with sparks
the coals embrace — By turns,
in craft, we're heard: Remarks
ignite the heart, excite
the soul... the art... the fight.

Free Will (It's All Neurons)

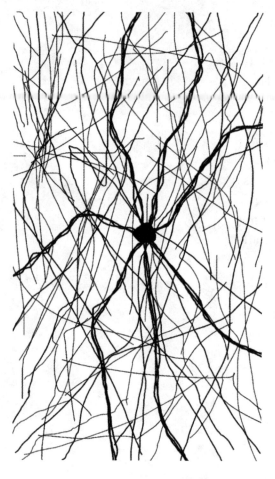

I'm all
I was.

It is
as it is.

A will
am I.

Flavours

I'm a muse,
to note,
raw at last:
salt,
aware to
notes umami....

Salt:
Warm, true seas to bite torment.

Sour:
A tart wine most battlers meet.

Bitter:
Sorrow's taste. A mute lament.

Umami:
Art, lost to art, between rests.

Sweet:
A stimulant; or (better) a storm.

Wavefunctions (It's All Observation)

LIPOGRAM

Speculation
authorises
perspicacious
mensuration —

instantaneously
encouraging
portraiture;
efficaciously
manoeuvring

repopulations.

Favourite
equations
communicate
equivocal,
simultaneous
behaviours....

AELINDROME

In spread
quantum views,
pitch dices
the ardent firmament.

Foams let
reality quake,
duet,
stage violins,
age violets.

Take duty!

Quiet realms
lament foam,
dent fires....
The arch dictum
views piquant,
read spin.

LORESCAPES

The Tower

Her eyes were red.
Her flesh and hair
were thin. The air
was thick with dread.
No hero, led
by love, was there
to scale that bare
and fragile thread.
For better truths,
our stories lied:
a broken flower,
the sickly youth
Rapunzel died
inside that tower.

A pure, lunar allure;
a paler upper pearl —
    reappear, a puzzle;
    lure an unreal leap.
        Pull up an earl,
        per a rare appeal....

Ever After

One sister cut off all her toes,
the other split her heel, to fit
the slipper, so the story goes.
A flock of doves would blind them. It
would leave them lost among the rows
and cobblestones — to crawl the grit
and grime, the wet and foetid street,
on searching hands and butchered feet.

CINDERELLA

Won, kill a hymn in me:
Loss. A will. A ball!
It tore boot, too....
Flee!
        Hot, stuck, sat one cinder's burn:
        Ella frets, is a fire he's in.
        Go certify, so care, play —
        O, royal, per a cosy fit, recognise her!
                If a sister, fallen, rubs red, nice not,
                ask cuts to heel, foot too be rot.
                        Till a ball,
                        I was solemn in my hall,
                        I know.

Beauty

BEGIN BEING

Bestowing beautiful belongings —
bedclothes, begonias, beads, bejewelled bearskins —
Belle's beastly benefactor behaves benevolently,
besides begging betrothment.
    Belle begins besieged, becomes bemused.
        Beauty, befooled, betrays beast,
        before, bereft, becoming besotted:
            Beneath beaming belvederes,
            becursed beastliness beholds Belle —
            belatedly beloved.

BEAUTY AND THE BEAST

Remove lore....
    Your sped,
    blue,
    clear beauty,
    one fire to me,
    instead be a drug.
    (This thug, dread beast in me!)
        To refine,
        you tear.
        Be a clue bled:
            Spur yore.
            Love more.

SPELL SLEEP

Young Briar Rose's wheel spins sleep,
there, under rage's faery curse....
       Until, years later, noble birth
       seeks Briar Rose's cheek,
       she'll dream among black skies,
       where omens creep.
              She'll enter lands
              where ruins speak....

BRIAR ROSE

Sleep's jaws seized beauty....
Charming squire, fix a kiss, to
liven Briar Rose.

Spinning Gold

THE WHEEL

RUMPELSTILTSKIN

So dreamt,
spin —
gold carats made....

A thread, then, is me!
Thus reason
enabled
the imp Rumpelstiltskin.

Wed is Misery!

She prods
a weave, a war —
"I leave awards!"
Awry,
she promises kin....

We dispel,
stilt —
the imp rumbled,
as one name,
thus read,
then is made
a threat.

Scars pin gold to dreams.

The Banshee

THE VIGIL

Peel, spirits!
  I mass, or call, a fine model.
  I awe bogeymen.
  I pillar, evoke, emote... I reel.
      I give now one vigil:
      Eerie-to-meek, over all I pine.
          My ego bewailed omen,
          I fall across a mist.
              I rip sleep.

THE SCREAM

This banshee seems
to know your home.
She drags her comb
across the beams.
Her skin like cream,
in monochrome,
she crawls the dome
and guides your dreams.
She falls to you.
Her claws are black
and stroke your cheek.
Her lips are blue,
but sharply crack —
to wail and shriek.

The Vampire

VESSELS

No smirch selfless,
ever a wan anaemic,
I rip.
        Maven,
          I wage bites sure of a foe.
              Russet,
              I beg a wine vampiric —
                  I mean:
                  an aware vessel,
                  flesh crimson....

CROOKED WINGS

A vampire lives alone.
She hates her crooked wings —
they drag along the stone.
A vampire lives alone.
Her spine a braid of bone,
she dreams of better things.
A vampire lives alone:
she hates her crooked wings.

Kelpies

LAKE

So alone,
madly,
lies a kelpie:
    Lakes' lily —
    a demon also.

LILIES

Sleek isles....
    Kelpies kill, like spies.
      Sleepless skies
      spill lipless kisses —
         lilies slip,
         else peel like silk.

The Wild Hunt

WRAITH

Wraith
impromptu.
Legion
devout....

FERNS

This fog: It spills
through blackened ferns.
The dead return
to haunt these hills;
their tumult chills
the air. As stern
as sorrow's burn,
their rattle fills
the mounting storm.
Their chant is out
of time. You sight
them, as they swarm
the earth, but doubt
they have the right.

Phantoms

THE HAUNTING

Because man forgets how to die,
we become fine ghosts — our data
but echoed afterimages. So, now,
come out, beget fear in shadows....

THE YEARNING

A bedroom
candle dims.
      Each flicker
      gradually halves
      its jewel,
      killing light.
Murky night
obliges phantoms,
quietly revealing
spirits.
      They unravel —
      veiled with xenogenesis;
      yearning zealously.

The Devil

THE EYE

Lived amiss,
I hide.
I burn my honeyed eye.
    No hymn rubied,
    I hiss.
        I'm a devil.

THE DARK

The devil met me in the dark.
He knew that he would find me there;
he saw that I had lost the spark.
The devil met me, in the dark.
He sunk a claw and made his mark,
and now I dwell forever where
the devil met me. In the dark,
he knew that he would find me there.

The Green Children of Woolpit

TWILIGHT

The Green Children of Woolpit
glow here, in the top cornfield,
fleeing their own, old crop: The
long, fine, epic Otherworld: The
dwelling, orphic-to-free, on the
lone perch of Eden or twilight....

DAWNING

The Green Children of Woolpit:
Here, their flesh grows too sick.
Here, the skies glow too bright....
Seek the hidden Moon tonight!
There, the innermost world joins
the sphere in the cosmos of light.

Godiva

THE COLT

Avid ogles made no garb....
I met sadness, elated a rapid idyll.
>A colt — eyed, untied — ordered no witness.
>>Eyes sent,
>>I wondered,
>>rode it nude,
>>yet locally did I parade....
>>>Tales send a stem, I brag —
>>>One damsel: Godiva.

THE STEED

A dare sets eyes
and sends revolution....
>Immodest or lowly,
>I am legally loosed,
>in protestation.
>>I ride a city,
>>undressed on a steed —
>>gadded, geed....
>>>I discredit a levy,
>>>demanding a law
>>>and a debt be repealed.

Avalon

No lava rose,
birth supine.

Vary,
eke no grail.
Meet so.

Ah, Celt!
Sacred art.

Punish!
On us, sun.

Oh, sin up, trader,
castle....

Chaos, *teem* —
liar gone.

Key raven,
I push tribes — or Avalon.

DEATH AND THE DOVE

As a Lancelot,
a vine hot,
Oberon's lie,
removed,
thus repays.

Pains —

King Arthur's cure recurs....

Hurt,
gain
skin.

Pay —

Spare us the dove,
Merlin's robe,
to hone vital ocean, alas.

Otherworld

I have not left, nor have I stayed.
The Otherworld has taken me.

I've slipped between the cracks we made;
I have not left, nor have I stayed.

Someday, you'll find me in the glade —
we'll meet beneath the knotted tree.

I have not left, nor have I stayed;
the Otherworld has taken me.

ENDSCAPES

Deathscape

Once, it was said that
death is in two acts: A
cessation, with data,
    and a white so static
    it can eat its shadow....

    Once, it was said that
    death is in two acts: A
    cessation, with data,
        and a white so static
        it can eat its shadow....

        Once, it was said that
        death is in two acts: A
        cessation, with data,
            and a white so static
            it can eat its shadow....

            Once, it was said that
            death is in two acts: A
            cessation, with data,
                and a white so static
                it can eat its shadow....

Death of the Sun, Moon, and Stars

Solar death sent a fey mob
to flame Earth's bays. Done,
the able, stray Moon fades,
beneath a melody of stars.

The sun
was dead
and done.

Each spark
we hold
goes dark:
The gold

It bled away in beams of dread and blue;
and shed its petal crescents, to the bone...
its core of metals melted — burned each hue
to red... The Moon is lost; its form and tone
a war of dust and black, beyond our view
of scores of lack.... Of course, the sky has known
of dearth before — but now its soul is tar...
so saw (did God) that space corrupts — Time scars.

the Earth
consumed
and doomed.

We're shown
no stars.

The Coffin

Mood sad,
lost I
a wan, if focal, life.

We rot.

Some rust nail,
posed under,
nooses a crack —
cuts a stuck carcase,
soon red....

Nude,
so pliant, sure,
most ore we fill —

A coffin awaits,
old as doom.

Oblivion

Oblivion will come for you.
It doesn't even know your name,

nor care to know. All debts accrue:
oblivion will come for you.

Indifferent is the solemn dew
that forms to quell the mortal flame.

Oblivion will come for you —
it doesn't even know your name.

End Times

POST APOCALYPSE I (FACEMASK)

Put it on.
Knot it up.
    Walks a man,
    in a mask....
        Law:
        Put it on.
        Knot it up.

POST APOCALYPSE II (SALT EARTH)

Tears halt
the altar's
latter ash.
    The astral
    rattle has
    her, at last.
        That's real —
        Salt earth.
        Salt Earth.

END OF DAYS I (DYSTOPIA)

Nowhere was truth less respected.
    Gradually,
    we humans,
    under persisting uncertainty,
    suffered.
        We struggled.
            We suffered uncertainty,
            persisting under humans
            we gradually respected less.
                Truth was nowhere.

END OF DAYS II (REVELATION)

The world was ending:
Dawn light worsened.
Nights wandered low.
The long wind was red
with drowned angels....

I Leave Torn

The Undertaker

[1]God removes his skull and folds it neatly by the stream.
The undertaker's missing valley sadly floods the tomb.
The devil folds mythology, struts bleakness in a dream.
A ghost refills the darkness. Day must, evidently, bloom....

[2]God removes his eyes and fills the tall but dormant sky.
The undertaker's bodies lift, all moved to glassy hymns.
The devil feasts, as demons darkly rustle moonlight by.
A flesh, long asked, returns to body mist. The valley dims.

[3]God removes his mystery, skin, and soul. The battled fall....
The undertaker lifts a ghastly elm, dissolved by moons.
The devil stays. A moody fog sinks thunder, trembles all.
The angels storm a vast, dim sky — refill the bloody dunes.

[4]God removes all time and sky, false trust, the holy binds.
The undertaker's atoms fall by void, else ghostly, minds.

Runically Unlyrical

Ragnarök

We, yonder, drag. Dim gods go flat. Anew,
the world is born, and twilight's petals bloom.
As elders fade, our fate is ever true.

Of Yggdrasil and dated Moon, we grew.
"Get Odin!" — dewy dawn, far daggers loom....
We yonder drag. Dim gods go flat, anew.

As evil fights, our flame is echoed through,
and even Frey owes fire its earthly tomb.
As elders fade, our fate is ever true.

We natal fogs dog Midgard — red, no yew.
Moods rise at all I kill — at Aesir's doom.
We, yonder, drag dim gods — go flat, anew.

A serpent damned, Jörmungandr reigned the blue
and ended braver Thor.... Guards seized the fume —
as elders fade, our fate is ever true.

By Fenrir, dead was Odin, so mist drew
to Surtur, Garm and Loki — to ones whom
we yonder drag. (Dim gods go flat, anew....)
As elders fade, our fate is ever true.

Chaos and Resurrection

VISUAL AELINDROME IN FEIGENBAUM'S FIRST CONSTANT

RIME ROYAL AELINDROME IN FEIGENBAUM'S FIRST CONSTANT

Go, neon eve — red seas dawn, as
a craw rots conscience.... Rid, He raised
last life. Now pale life, spun at, has
a maze. Dead sent, dead seas amazed.
       He spun a tale — "Lift life, now praised!"
       Lashed, science riots. Con raw dawn —
       a sacred season, ever gone....

RIME ROYAL ANAGRAM

End, nova, in that fierce sea-flame.
Nailed echoes loose a seizure dense:
an answer, in disorder's game
of raised and rapid resonance.
       Space, cast of awe and decadence,
       let chaos gaze a shapeless view,
       till stardust spawns a world anew.

Omegas

Alpha and Omega

A gem, on word, lived apart.
Pagan omega has me hewn.

I, alpha dog, deed God.

Ah, plain, we hems! —
Ah, a gem!
On a gap, trap a devil —
drown omega.

```
A G E M O N W O R D
L I V E D A P A R T
P A G A N O M E G A
H A S M E H E W N I
A L P H A D O G D E
E D G O D A H P L A
I N W E H E M S A H
A G E M O N A G A P
T R A P A D E V I L
D R O W N O M E G A
```

War Ends War

Tao may be now a sign I knell afar.
A wasted act in killing is to die.
To newer awe, be sure now, onward eye.
Defer old loss — I kill it. So, I mar....

It's one to me, revolt: a devil's tar.
Erupt it. Fight life. Rot. Dirt up, I lie.
Vast sacredness, raw rats, a noose I tie —
of redder foe, I tie so, on a star.

War's sender casts a veil I, putrid, tore.
Filth! Gift it. Pure rats lived at love remote.
No stir, am I — O, still I kiss old lore.

Fed eye, draw now. "One ruse beware," we note.
I dot.... Sign ill. I knit cadets a war.
A fallen king? I saw one, by a moat....

ANAGRAM TWO: SHAKESPEAREAN

Due fits: *I, myriad. I, brutal war*....
Bone, dull as air, asserts I'm still a cog,
to rise in Eden ivy, raw as raw.
No wedded rage remote — soon, it's a fog.

To hostile war! A faker tier: *I, fleets.*
We note no law — O, vast in evil's knit....
I pote lorn rot. Deeps tall, I knife deceit.
Tie, cede. *Fin.* Kill at speed — torn, role to pit.

Inks liven. It's a vow, alone-to-new.
Steel fire, I trek afar — awe lit so hot.
Go fast: I noose, to me, regarded dew.
On, war's a wary vine — denies I rot.

"Go call its mistress!" arias allude.
No brawl; a turbid, airy mist: *I, feud.*

FORMSCAPES

Slate Petals (and Other Wordscapes) is a work of experimental and traditional formal poetry. The book's subject is form itself: forms of nature and forms of thought; external and internal landscapes.

Like its prequel—*Stray Arts (and Other Inventions)* (Penteract Press, 2019)—*Slate Petals* looks to three key areas of formalism: Poems that adhere to fixed rhyme schemes and prescribed metrical patterns; poems heavily constrained by alphabetical or lexical requirements; and visual poems, composed via the spatial manipulation of symbols (be these symbols letters, nonverbal glyphs, or more intricate images).

In *Stray Arts*, the *limits* of combinatorial formalism were tested. Its anagrammatic and palindromic metrical verse, in particular, walked the line between meaning and nonmeaning—occasionally foregoing the former to highlight instead those curious linguistic micro-structures that can arise from within a macrostructure's tyranny. The book's central statement was that a poem's architecture, and not its textual content, can often be its primary aesthetic drive.

Following this, *Slate Petals* turns its attention to the *range* of formalism, from poem-as-lyric to poem-as-structure. Its visual poetry goes from traditional calligrams to asemic pattern poems to the entirely nontextual. Its verse includes short formal poems (with meanings, metres, and rhyme schemes as lucid as those of nursery rhymes); lengthier poems that obey the strictures and music of tested, conventional forms; and severely restricted poems, striving for the lyrical in spite of their shackles. There are also more elaborate, experimental structures: poems interlocking simple verse forms within a grander, premeditated architecture and sets of poems determining each other's content at the levels of letter, word, and theme, as well as several rigorous explorations into the complexities of combinatorial constraint—experiments into the breakdown of language, embracing the art of *form for form's sake*.

With a special focus on types of palindrome, anagram, and sonnet, *Slate Petals* joins *Stray Arts* in examining that which lies between the lyrical or conversational aspects of poetry and the poet's geometric ideals—between meaning and music; between writing and drawing; between feeling and form.

Landscapes

THE DESERT
A palindrome-by-letter, prefaced by a short palindrome-by-pairs (a palindrome that is palindromic by blocks of two letters, as in the phrase "reside in desire": re-si-de-in-de-si-re).

THE WONDER
A palindrome-by-letter and an anagram-poem (a poem whose lines are perfect anagrams of each other).

TIME TURNS THE SHADOWS
Two palindromes-by-letter that use the exact same letter set (i.e., two perfectly anagrammed palindromes). Beneath them is a thematically related palindrome-by-word.

COLOURSCAPE
An ottava rima (ABABABCC) in iambic pentameter, intersected by a Shakespearean sonnet in iambic monometer—such that the third metrical foot of each line of the ottava rima belongs also to the sonnet. It is preceded by an anagram-poem.

LANDSCAPE
A lipogram-sonnet—in iambic dimeter and adhering to the Shakespearean rhyme scheme—that uses only the eight different letters of its title: l, a, n, d, s, c, p and e.

THE DALES

An aelindrome—obeying the repeated sequence 1-2-3-4, to 20 figures (12341234123412341234)—accompanied by a palindrome-by-pairs. [Note: The aelindrome is a restriction whose formal definition was first introduced in *Stray Arts (and Other Inventions)*—a definition that is repeated later in this book (pages 143-144).]

MOUNTAIN RANGE TRIOLET

An asemic poem whose "lines" are horizons, tracing the points at which various mountain ranges meet the sky. The poem is a triolet, in that it replicates the repeated lines of a textual triolet: ABAAABAB, or (putting rhyme aside) 12314512. The lines are, in order: Alps, Himalayas, Andes, Alps, Karakoram, Sierra Nevada, Alps, Himalayas. The lines were traced from stock images found online.

THE HILLS

A palindrome-by-letter and an anagram-poem.

CROWSCAPES

Four poems: a palindrome-by-letter; a triolet in iambic tetrameter; an anagram-poem; and a Shakespearean sonnet in iambic monometer.

BEES ON THE FERTILE HEATH

An aelindrome in the first 8 digits of the golden ratio (16180339), prefacing a rudimentary calligram consisting of a palindrome-by-letter and an anagram-poem.

MATHEMATICS OF A FROZEN LAKE

A palindromic haiku, followed by an aelindrome in the first 17 digits of the natural logarithm of 2 (ln2): 06931471805599453.

WINTERSCAPES

Three poems: an anagram-poem, a palindrome-by-letter, and a second anagram-poem.

WINTER SOLSTICE

Four six-line poems, each constrained by the term "winter solstice." The first poem is a homovocalism, whose lines employ the same vowels, in the same order, while varying consonants. The second poem consists of perfectly anagrammed lines. The third poem is a lipogram, whose lines use only the ten letters of "winter solstice": w, i, n, t, e, r, s, o, l, and c. Each line of the fourth poem consists of a six-letter word followed by an eight-letter word.

THE WOODS ARE DEEP

A visual poem making symmetrical patterns from a desaturated photograph. The original photograph (overleaf) was taken by the author in woods near the author's home.

LEAVES

A palindrome-by-letter and a triolet in iambic tetrameter.

CITY SCAFFOLD

A blank verse sonnet in iambic trimeter. Each line has exactly 14 letters. Moreover, among the 196 (14^2) letters, the poem's Ts are positioned such that they form an X-shape through the sonnet (as represented beside the poem).

CITYSCAPE

A palindromic haiku, followed by a Shakespearean sonnet, in iambic dimeter, that is composed only of four-letter words (tetragrams).

NAME THIS WORLD

"Name This World" begins with a lipogrammatic palindrome-by-letter about a failed cartographer. The palindrome uses only the 13 letters of the phrase "name this world."

This palindrome is followed by an *imperfect* anagram, which reassembles the palindrome's letters, but incorrectly (that is, the two poems "fail to map"). Though all the consonants of the palindrome (n, m, t, h, s, w, r, l, and d) are perfectly anagrammed, the vowels are muddled: while the palindrome has four es and 12 as, the "anagram" has 12 es and four as; and while the palindrome has six os and 11 is, the "anagram" has 11 os and six is.

Seascapes

<u>MARINA</u>
A palindrome-by-letter and an anagram-poem.

<u>THE GULLS</u>
A palindrome-calligram and a Petrarchan sonnet in iambic monometer.

<u>ASEMIC TALES OF A COASTAL SLATE</u>
A desaturated, brightened, and highly sharpened photograph of a piece of slate from the North Welsh coast—detailing the asemic writing of metamorphic formation and coastal erosion.

<u>WAVESCAPE</u>
A Shakespearean sonnet, in iambic dimeter, composed such that it can be split down its centre to produce both an iambic monometer Shakespearean sonnet and an iambic monometer Petrarchan sonnet.

<u>THE MAIN</u>
Four sonnets that are perfect anagrams of each other. All are in iambic dimeter. Three of the sonnets obey the Shakespearean rhyme scheme, while the fourth is Petrarchan. Moreover, the third sonnet is also a palindrome-by-letter. Two of these sonnets are named for mythology-inspired phrasal anagrams and two are named for warships.

<u>THE SEA-SERPENT</u>
An erasure poem, partially erasing text from page 106 of *The Great Sea-Serpent: An Historical and Critical Treatise* by Anthonie Cornelis Oudemans (1892).

ABOVE AND BELOW
A triolet in iambic tetrameter, preceded by an aelindrome in π (to 11 significant figures: 31415926535).

THE ISLAND
A palindrome-by-letter and a Shakespearean sonnet in iambic dimeter.

Skyscapes

EARLY MOON
An anagram-poem.

EARLY SUN
An anagram-poem, reproducing the lyrical tone and formal style "Early Moon" employed.

THE CLOUDS
A palindrome-by-triples, prefacing a triolet in iambic tetrameter.

THE SCATTERING
A poem about the Earth's atmosphere's scattering of sunlight—and an experiment in "metrical scattering":

Each of the poem's three quatrains is in tetrameter. Moreover, in each stanza, the second and third lines rhyme and the fourth line twice repeats the first two metrical feet of the first line. However, the metrical feet of the three quatrains differ—the feet lengthening by one unstressed syllable each successive quatrain. Thus, the first quatrain uses iambs (x/), the second quatrain uses amphibrachs (x/x), and the third quatrain uses tertius paeons (xx/x).

DOVE OF PIECES

A monometer Petrarchan sonnet, each line of which ends with the letters "ove." The sonnet is accompanied by a visual poem made from Minion Pro, the typeface used throughout this book.

THE DEPARTURE

A triolet, in iambic pentameter, intersected by a Shakespearean sonnet in iambic monometer—such that one metrical foot of each line of the triolet belongs also to the sonnet. This poem is preceded by a palindrome-by-pairs.

NEAR SIDE OF THE MOON

An anagram-poem, followed by a Petrarchan sonnet in iambic monometer.

FAR SIDE OF THE MOON

A palindrome-by-letter, followed by a homovocalic poem (whose lines use the same vowels, in the same order).

LUNAR PHASES SESTINA

Six phases of the Moon—waxing gibbous, first quarter, waxing crescent, waning gibbous, last quarter, and waning crescent—permuted according to the end-word pattern of sestina form.

MOON IN A WATERFALL

Two palindromes—the first by word and the second by letter.

YOUR STAR

A Shakespearean sonnet, in iambic dimeter, that consists only of four-letter words (tetragrams).

I LOVE THE STARS

A Petrarchan sonnet in iambic tetrameter.

THE COMET, AT MIDNIGHT

A Shakespearean sonnet in iambic pentameter.

THE SMALLEST STARS
A Shakespearean sonnet in iambic hexameter.

NOIR OF ORION
Symmetrical visual poetry made from non-overlapping glyphs of the constellation Orion.

THE LITERATURE OF STARS
A villanelle in iambic pentameter.

PALIMPSEST
A sonnet in iambic tetrameter, with the unconventional sonnet form ABBABAABCDECDE.

Mindscapes

JULY
An ottava rima in iambic pentameter.

SOLEMN
The first stanza of "Solemn" is a palindrome-by-letter. The second stanza is a homovocalism of the first stanza—that is, it uses the same vowels, in the same order, but changes the consonants. It is thus palindromic in its vowels only. The third stanza is a homoconsonantism of the first stanza—it uses the same consonants, in the same order, but changes the vowels. It is thus palindromic in its consonants only.

TRIONNET
A poem that, depending on where its line breaks occur, can be read either as a sonnet in iambic tetrameter or as a triolet in iambic heptameter. The trionnet's rhyme, repetition, and stress scheme is presented opposite (in its triolet form), with x and y denoting repeated lines, u representing unstressed syllables, S representing stressed syllables, and A to G representing (stressed) rhymes:

uSuAuBuCuSuDuE - [x]
uFuSuGuSuCuSuG - [y]
uSuFuSuSuSuEuE
uSuAuBuCuSuDuE - [x]
uSuSuSuBuSuSuE
uAuSuSuSuDuDuG
uSuAuBuCuSuDuE - [x]
uFuSuGuSuCuSuG - [y]

VERSESCAPES
Four poems: an anagram-poem; a lipogram-sonnet, in iambic dime-
ter, that employs only six letters; a palindrome-by-pairs; and an
acrostic sonnet in iambic monometer.

A VILLANELLE
A villanelle in iambic dimeter.

LOVE SONNET OF THE CAUTIOUS ROMANTIC
A Shakespearean sonnet in iambic tetrameter.

NEW INK
A usable typeface—programmed as a TrueType font file (.ttf)—
designed specifically for this book. Its letters are presented here both
in alphabetical order (columns 1 and 2) and in the order in which they
appear on a qwerty keyboard, left to right, top to bottom (columns 3
and 4).

KNIT INK
Preceded by a palindrome-by-letter, "Knit Ink" presents two rime
royals (scheme: ABABBCC); one is in iambic tetrameter, the other is in
iambic trimeter. The poems are connected by a Shakespearean sonnet
in iambic monometer, each line of which makes up a metrical foot in
one of the two rime royals.

THIS STATUS IS JOY
A perfect anagram of the poem "This Is Just to Say" by William Carlos Williams.

THE RAVEN
Inspired by the notion that, for its many virtues, Edgar Allan Poe's "The Raven" is overly long, this "distillation" uses permutational methods to reduce Poe's 18 stanzas to three (while preserving the original's stanzaic form). The metre is similarly simplified to a sequence of uniform trochees (with catalexis). Moreover, the abbreviated poem uses only words that appear in Poe's original (albeit permitting pluralised and singularised noun forms).

LAMENTS OF A CARVED WOODEN OWL
A palindrome-by-letter, followed by a Petrarchan sonnet in iambic dimeter.

DREAMS OF A PAPER SWAN
A palindrome-by-pairs, followed by four 5-7-5 syllable count haiku that are perfect anagrams of each other.

WANTS OF AN AGEING DOLL
A palindrome-by-letter, followed by a triolet in iambic tetrameter.

THOUGHTS OF A HUMAN ADRIFT
A palindrome-by-word, followed by a triolet in iambic tetrameter.

THE ALCHEMIST
An anagram-poem, prefacing a set of three short anagrammed texts.

In these anagrammed texts, a "source text"—presented in all caps—is anagrammed twice, creating two cascading 10-word poems. The first of these 10-word poems features words beginning with the letters a a e d f c b a a b. These letters' values—given a=1, b=2, c=3, etc.—add up to 26, the atomic number of iron. The second 10-word poem has words beginning with the letters c g f a c b b t p s, whose values, by the same method, add up to 79—the atomic number of gold.

AN INCANTATION
Three palindromes-by-letter that use the exact same set of letters (i.e., three perfectly anagrammed palindromes). The three poems, in turn, descend deeper into the obscurant language associated with both mystical incantations and strictly constrained verse.

OF MUSIC AND MEMORY
Two poems: "Distant Music" is an ottava rima in iambic tetrameter and also a palindrome. "Distant Memory" is a triolet in iambic tetrameter and also a perfect anagram of "Distant Music."

MARIONETTE NOIR A.M.
A 20-second musical palindrome, intended for harpsicord.

THEATRESCAPES
Three poems: a palindrome-by-pairs, an anagram-poem, and a haiku that uses only words that contain the letters 'the' in order.

DRINKS FOR DIONYSUS
An anagram-poem, followed by a palindrome-by-letter.

OF WINE AND WORDS
What might be called a "nesting doll sonnet": The complete poem is a Shakespearean sonnet in iambic trimeter. However, if only the first two iambs of each line are read, it becomes a Spenserian Sonnet in iambic dimeter. Similarly, if only the first iamb of each line is read, it becomes a Petrarchan sonnet in iambic monometer.

FREE WILL (IT'S ALL NEURONS)
An asemic poem of hastily scrawled lines, sketching out an improvised neuron. This visual poem is accompanied by a palindrome-by-letter.

FLAVOURS
A palindrome-by-letter, prefacing a sequence of five anagrammed statements.

WAVEFUNCTIONS (IT'S ALL OBSERVATION)

A "reverse lipogram," permitting only words that contain all five of the letters a, e, i, o, and u. It is accompanied by an aelindrome in π^e, thus the sequence 22459157718361045473.

Lorescapes

THE TOWER
A Petrarchan sonnet in iambic dimeter, followed by a lipogram using only the letters r, a, p, u, n, z, e, and l.

EVER AFTER
An ottava rima in iambic tetrameter, followed by a palindrome-by-letter.

BEAUTY
Two poems about "Beauty and the Beast" and two poems about "Briar Rose." The first dyad consists of a double tautogram—all of whose words begin with the letters "be"—and a palindrome-by-pairs. The second dyad consists of a poem that uses only five-letter words (pentagrams) and a pangram-haiku (which uses every letter of the alphabet at least once).

SPINNING GOLD
Two aelindromes: one visual, one textual.

Beginning with a simple glyph of the "golden spiral," the visual aelindrome presents a form derived from angular permutations determined by the decimal expansion of the golden ratio. To create it, the golden spiral was first positioned at 1 degree from the horizontal (since the first digit of the golden ratio is 1), before being replicated at 7 degrees (i.e., a further 6 degrees up, since the golden ratio's second digit is 6), and so on, until the 90-degree point was crossed. At this point, the golden ratio's decimal expansion was reversed, and each digit of the golden ratio, in turn, back to its first, added to the angle. On an aesthetic whim, the result was then reproduced in white, at 2/3 size, and pasted over the larger structure. The entire work was then, in a statement of pure symmetry, reflected vertically—and complemented by a found sketch of a spinning wheel (artist unknown).

The textual aelindrome is similarly composed in the decimal expansion of the golden ratio, whose sequence is here taken to twenty digits: 16180339887498948482.

THE BANSHEE
A palindrome-by-letter, followed by a Petrarchan sonnet in iambic dimeter.

THE VAMPIRE
A palindrome-by-letter, followed by a triolet in iambic trimeter.

KELPIES
A palindrome-by-pairs, followed by a lipogram-poem, which uses only the letters k, e, l, p, i, and s.

THE WILD HUNT
A Petrarchan sonnet in iambic dimeter, prefaced by a minimalist double acrostic consisting of four words whose first and last letters together spell out "wild hunt."

PHANTOMS
An anagram-poem and an abecedarian poem (whose words' first letters follow the alphabet).

THE DEVIL
A palindrome-by-letter, followed by a triolet in iambic tetrameter.

THE GREEN CHILDREN OF WOOLPIT
Inspired by a strange medieval legend from the village of Woolpit in Suffolk, this dyad consists of an anagram-poem and a homovocalic poem (whose lines use the same vowels, in the same order).

GODIVA
A dyad retelling the legend of Lady Godiva via two complementary, first-person accounts—one past tense and one present tense. The first account is a palindrome-by-letter and the second is a perfect anagram of this palindrome.

AVALON

Two palindromes inspired by Arthurian legend—the first is a palindrome-by-letter and the second is a palindrome-by-pairs. The two palindromes are perfect anagrams of each other.

OTHERWORLD

A triolet in iambic tetrameter.

Endscapes

DEATHSCAPE

An anagram-poem, repeated to disintegration.

DEATH OF THE SUN, MOON, AND STARS

An ottava rima in iambic pentameter (Moon), sharing the first foot of each line with a monometer Spenserian sonnet (Sun) and the last foot of each line with a monometer Shakespearean-Petrarchan hybrid sonnet (ABABCDCDCDEEDE, Stars). It is prefaced by an anagram-poem.

THE COFFIN

A palindrome-by-letter.

OBLIVION

A triolet in iambic tetrameter.

END TIMES

Four poems: a palindrome-by-letter, a poem of anagrammed lines, a palindrome-by-word, and a second anagram-poem.

I LEAVE TORN

A visual poem, made from three torn papyri fragments, each discovered in Oxyrhynchus, Egypt, during the late nineteenth or early twentieth century. The fragments contain passages from the Book of Revelation, in Greek. These fragments have been replicated, resized, and flipped, in order to piece together a self-guided jigsaw puzzle.

THE UNDERTAKER

An anagram-sonnet (anagrammed lines), in iambic heptameter, whose stanzas each begin with an acephalous line, the first foot of which consists only of the same single, stressed syllable: "God."

RUNICALLY UNLYRICAL

An asemic concrete palindrome, built from the Norse futhark alphabet.

RAGNARÖK

A villanelle, in iambic pentameter, each stanza of which employs a different literary restriction. These restrictions, under the overarching constraint of villanelle form, impact upon each other, such that each stanza ultimately obeys not an isolated rule, but rather a composite rule determined, in part, by the strictures of its neighbours. The rules for each stanza are:

1—Each line has eight words.
2—Anagrammed lines (same letters, different order).
3—By line, corresponding words begin with the same letter (the first word of each line begins with a, the second with e, etc.).
4—A palindrome-by-letter.
5—Homovocalic lines (same vowels, same order).
6—By line, corresponding words have the same letter count (the first word of each line has two letters, the second six, etc.).

CHAOS AND RESURRECTION

A visual aelindrome, made the same way as the aelindrome from "Spinning Gold"—but with angular permutations determined by Feigenbaum's first constant, and with a bifurcation diagram (whose form is determined by Feigenbaum's first constant) as its source glyph.

This visual aelindrome is followed by two textual poems: The first poem obeys the rime royal form, is composed in iambic tetrameter, and is an aelindrome in Feigenbaum's first constant—thus, in 4669201609102990671853. The second poem obeys the rime royal form, is composed in iambic tetrameter, and is a perfect anagram of the aelindromic rime royal.

<u>OMEGAS</u>
An asemic palindrome built from hastily hand-drawn omegas.

<u>ALPHA AND OMEGA</u>
A palindrome further constrained both by a partial acrostic and by its adherence to a 10 by 10 letter grid.

<u>WAR ENDS WAR</u>
Two palindromic sonnets in iambic pentameter. The first sonnet is Petrarchan; the second is Shakespearean. The two sonnets are perfect anagrams of each other.

Concision and Constraint

Many of the forms in this collection are short. The triolet uses only eight lines, as does the ottava rima. Rime royals make do with seven lines; haiku only three. The majority of the sonnets in this book are in either monometer or dimeter, and the palindromic and anagrammatic poems here are generally shorter than those of *Stray Arts*.

Constraint and concision go well together. The most stringent literary restrictions, such as palindromes, are more manageable when kept short. There is, in addition to this, an elegance to brevity that neatly complements the idealism of a structural conceit.

In celebration of this book's tendency towards concision, I am here including a series of single-line constrained works. Not all necessarily "poems," these pieces nonetheless employ the same techniques used throughout both *Slate Petals* and *Stray Arts*:

PALINDROMES-BY-LETTER
The pithy palindrome is a favourite of puzzlers and constraint-based writers. Probably my best-known one-liner is this, a set of instructions on how to draw a pyramid:

A zig. Now one zag. Gaze now on Giza!

Another of my best is this, about the Battle of Bosworth Field:

Drowsy brawl. A York royal. War by sword.

Here are a few others:

No omen of Orion, mid a dim noir of one Moon....

Define my ego: Obese boogeymen I fed.

Rein a zebra. Career a car. Be zanier.

Emote me, rule me, be me — lure me to me

Tire my rare tillage, regal literary merit!

Won't some dice decide most now?

Pull a music: I pen an epic. I sum all up.

So: genial lives oppose villain egos.

May a root atop a moor groom a potato or a yam?

I, maniacs, send Abel Bible badness.... Cain am I.

A repose suffuses order as a red rose suffuses opera.

Beware: venom mustn't summon ever a web.

No one vital erases a relative noon.

Spill a poem and name opal lips.

Sonar poses, or solos, rose sopranos.

"Emotion? I'm odd; a mad domino." — I, to me.

A mardy doom asserts I stress a moody drama.

Wonder erases order: Non-red roses are red now.

No omega vast, solar, or a lost savage moon....

PALINDROMES-BY-PAIRS (AND ONE BY-TRIPLES)

Palindromes-by-pairs lend themselves just as well to the one-liner. Here are some of mine:

A drone, lost, lay, as by a last, lone road.

By ruins, trees rest, in ruby.

We save lost love's awe.

In past love, half have lost pain.

A dream sighs — I am read.

Intense ion, Einstein!

We don't desire a president, do we?

And one palindrome-by-triples:

May disorder wonder word dismay.

ANAGRAMS

There are various types of short anagram—anagrammed names being a popular one. A very pleasing phenomenon is the "phrasal anagram"—the titles "Poisoned Poseidon," "Risen Siren," "Begin Being," and "Runically Unlyrical," from this collection, as well as "Remote Meteor" from *Stray Arts*, are favourite examples.

Pithy prose anagrams can also be made from pairs of sentences, or from a string of clauses. Here's an example of each (I consider these among my best):

Shot a salted seabird. The albatross is dead.

The rain, then air, are thin, in earth....

PANGRAMS

The pangram is a constraint that demands concision—this is especially true of the isopangram, whose stipulation is that each letter of the alphabet be used once and *only* once. Here's my best effort (to be presented alongside an appropriate .jpg image, of course):

> *Crwth.jpg — Vex, quiz my folk bands!*

Given the difficulty of writing isopangrams, I have experimented with loosening the restriction a little. For example, this pangram—a variant on the above—allows two extra letters (an additional u and an additional i):

> *Crwth jig and pub quiz vex my folks....*

And this pangram uses every letter of the alphabet only once—apart from a, which is used six times:

> *My jackdaw flaps, heaving a quartz box.*

Finally, these pangrams use a, e, i, o and u exactly twice, but every other letter exactly once:

> *A quick, brown fox jumps the glazed ivy.*

> *Webs of mock plight quiz and vex a jury.*

Regarding the Aelindrome

The aelindrome is a new constraint, which I devised during the autumn of 2012, after discovering the possibility and potential of "palindromes-by-pairs" ("Intense? I am Einstein!"). Aelindromes (derived from my initials: A. E.-lindromes) are a variation on traditional palindromes—however, instead of mirroring a repeated, fixed letter-unit, they reverse units of variable sizes, as determined by premeditated numerical sequences. That is, while palindromes-by-letter and palindromes-by-pairs use consistent, *homogeneous* units (1 and 2, respectively), aelindromes employ *heterogeneous* units, variously grouped according to underlying numerical palindromes.

An example: the phrase "Melody, a bloody elm" is an aelindrome structured by the numerical palindrome 1234321, since $[m]_1$ $[el]_2$ $[ody]_3$ $[a blo]_4$ reflects backward as $[a blo]_4$ $[ody]_3$ $[el]_2$ $[m]_1$. By convention, aelindromes are said to be "in" the forward incarnation of their sequence (up to and including its pivot). Thus, "Melody, a bloody elm" is an "aelindrome in 1234."

Note that, when parsing letters this way, a unit of zero letters will return as a unit of zero letters—absence reflects as absence. Thus, an aelindrome in 1234 has a structure identical to that of an aelindrome in, for example, 10020300000004.

By my technical definition of the aelindrome, word-unit palindromes that obey premeditated letter numbers—e.g., "I am mad, am I?" [12321]—while superficially aelindromic, cannot rightly be considered aelindromes. A palindrome cannot simultaneously adhere to homogeneous and heterogeneous units of palindromy. Put another way, the word-unit palindromism of such palindromes *overrules* any claim to aelindromism: Just as it would be absurd to call palindromes-by-letter "aelindromes in 111 (etc.)" or palindromes-by-pairs "aelindromes in 222 (etc.)," a word-unit palindrome that is patterned after premeditated letter numbers is merely a special case of palindrome-by-word (it is a palindrome-by-word that follows an additional letter-count restriction).

Aelindromes, then, cannot be palindromes. They exhibit palindromic bidirectionality in the numerical sequences underpinning them, but *never even the possibility* of bidirectionality in a consistent linguistic unit (letter, word, line, sentence, paragraph, etc.). Aelindromes have palindromic bones, but not palindromic skin. By this fact, there can be no "word-unit aelindromes" at all, since it is always possible for grouped words to be coherently redistributed into lines—thus making any apparent word-unit aelindrome merely a restitched line-unit palindrome (with specified, reflected word counts for each line, as in symmetrical pattern poetry). Similar applies to lines and to stanzas; it follows that, as a textual exercise, aelindromes are an inherently and unambiguously letter-based constraint.

In this collection, the poem "The Dale" constructs an aelindrome from the repeated sequence 1-2-3-4. The other aelindromes in *Slate Petals* are aelindromic in the decimal expansions of the golden ratio (φ), the natural logarithm of 2 (ln2), pi (π), pi to the power of Euler's number (π^e), and Feigenbaum's first constant (δ). A breakdown of one of this book's aelindromes is opposite.

Mathematics of a Frozen Lake
(Aelindrome in the Decimal Expansion of
the Natural Logarithm of 2)

6931471805599453

[Rested]₆ [ice
pools c]₉[old]₃ [f]₁[lake]₄[s
now
on a]₇ [w]₁[inter's la]₈ [ke.

I ce]₅[ment a]₅ [thematic o]₉[asis;
see ma]₉[in ab]₄[aci,
al]₅ [l gl]₃[acial]₅,
[in a b]₄[asis —
see ma]₉[thematic o]₉[men ta]₅[ke.

Ice]₅ [inters la]₈[w]₁.

[Snow, on a]₇ [lake]₄!
[F]₁[old]₃ [ice,
pools c]₉[rested]₆....

Praise for *Slate Petals (and Other Wordscapes)*

"The world needs Anthony Etherin, whose fascination with language —particularly anagrams, palindromes and sonnets—has inspired him to create poems like none that have been seen before. Sometimes bizarre, occasionally obscure, they can also be strangely beautiful. And they're always fascinating. I'm a great admirer of his work."
                                        —Anthony Horowitz

"Anthony Etherin does it again! He continues to render all my own virtuoso ventures obsolete. I truly covet this book even more than its prequel."
                                        —Christian Bök

"Anthony Etherin's heroic explorations of the possibilities of poetry engendered by order imposed on the apparently random lead him to ever more fertile territory. Anagrams, palindromes and countless variations on such things establish a landscape of lyrical and magical coincidences. It is not so much that such things can be done at all but that they propose a condition between the will to make and the will to discover. The poem is in the patterns in the grass."
                                        —George Szirtes

Material from this book has previously appeared in the chapbooks *Danse Macabre* (above/ground press, 2018), *Quartets* (Penteract Press, 2019), *Otherworld* (no press, 2019), and *Thaumaturgy* (above/ground press, 2020).

Ten poems in this collection are adaptations of poems from the book *Cellar* (Penteract Press, 2018).

In addition: Sections of the poems "Time Turns the Shadows," "Cityscape," "Solemn," and "The Devil" appeared in the anthology *Reflections* (Penteract Press, 2019). The combinatorial formal poem from "Colourscape" and the poem "Wavescape" were previously published online together as "Spacescapes" (IceFloe Press, 2020). Parts of "Crowscapes" appeared in the leaflet "The Crows" (The Blasted Tree, 2018). "City Scaffold" and "An Incantation" were published online by The Pi Review (2020). "The Gulls" appeared in Antilang. magazine (no. 2, 2018). An early version of "The Sea-Serpent" was first published in the anthology *Myth & Metamorphosis* (Penteract Press, 2020). "The Clouds" was quoted for Sébastien Hildebrand's book *Clouds* (Timglaset / Plaugolt Satzwechsler, 2021). "I Love the Stars" and "The Literature of Stars" previously appeared in the anthology *Science Poems* (Penteract Press, 2020). "This Status Is Joy" previously appeared in the anthology *Concrete & Constraint* (Penteract Press, 2018). "Godiva" was first published as a nano-pamphlet (Penteract Press, 2018). Part of "End Times" appeared in *The Daily Telegraph* (August 30th, 2020). "I Leave Torn" features in the anthology *The Mouth of a Lion* (Steel Incisors, 2021). And "War Ends War" was first published as a leaflet (Enneract Editions, 2020).

THE NOSON
SONNETS

ANTHONY ETHERIN

The Noson Sonnets

OTHER WORLDS 5

THE REIN THEREIN 9

PALINONNETS 13

AELINSCAPES 17

NOTES 21

Noson
yn y ddydd.
Ddydd
yn y noson.

Other Worlds

ANNWN

At night, the woodland scatters lunar rays
astride that point where this world and the next
become each other's shadows. In the haze,
a crooked wreath of branches frames a text
composed of living leaves and roses dead.

The Otherworld is written into ours
when, deep within its kingdom, ours is read.

The crawling fae beget themselves, like stars,
and slither up the roots of elder oaks
malformed, before the moonlight chisels flesh
with all the passion mortal lore invokes —
from beauties old as art to horrors fresh.

The other world is bled to yours and mine,
in forms of love and evil we design.

GHOST

In death, you puncture darkness, never days.
Against this night, faint dust moves low and pale.
Occult, your phases flutter to our gaze.
I capture shapes in fleeting spells. I fail,
resigned to fathom shroud but never core.

How incomplete my essence that, alas,
your full return was missing from my lore.

Now strained, the After obfuscates *your* glass:
You witness me, yet brief is every view.
(Adjoining worlds are moonbeams trading light;
they mix our shadows, moving ever through.)
Your glimpses see me fey, my glimmer white....

How empty, vague we look in death; yet here,
I'm misty to *your* eye — just my veneer.

The Rein Therein

SO MEMO ON

Howl — unabated, nigh — the reins of art.
Here, in so fair a lighted season, cede
ephemeral, unable dares. Cue start.
Or end: crode some tomes in sweeping reeds.

Old ark, ensemble mask below constraint....
Herein seduce the sea. I'm still ashore.
The rending olden sky, lines' flowless paint,
herein is limit's idled ash — adore!

Forms memo on, be ambled tomes in glow;
bewilder comet onyx, slight of eye.
Art hones our gentle ash decrees, ink low.
Lines sate the rending. Nigh, the reins untie.

So merited is order's tar: Red. Scarred.
Sidereal. A sword. A shot. A shard.

SOME MOON

How Luna bated night here — insofar
the reins of air alighted seas once deep....
Hemera! Luna bled a rescue star
to render ode. So, me to me, sins weep.

In greed, Sol darkens. Emblem, ask, "Be low:
constrain the reins, educe these aims, till ash
or ether end in golden skylines' flow...."

Less pain therein, I slim its idle dash.
Ado reforms me. Moonbeam bled to me,
"Sing low. Be wilder. Come to Nyx's light!"
O, fey Earth, one so urgent, leash decree;
sink lowliness, a tether ending night.

Here, in Sun, tie some rite disorder starred.
Scar red side, real as word: As hot. As hard.

Palinonnets

MOONLESS NIGHT

The dark was born, bejewelled with elder lights
that sparkled gently through its massing cloud.
(It spoke, to say it feared such moonless nights....)
Below, the earth was bowing in its shroud.

Then smoke, each fibre grieving, loomed on high:
a crow ascending, blotting out each star.
Its char of wings now spread across the sky;
denial, loss, and deader things afar.

This tar of doubt — this rot — was ended so,
when twilight bloomed to weave a vibrant cloak.
Dawn's crowd, beginning now to birth a glow,
grew bright — and soon it neared: the day awoke.

Sun, proud and passing truly, sent its mark.
Its rites beheld and fuelled the morning lark.

DANCERS AFTER DARK

A fearless darkness wakes arenas dead:
The pale and dear departed dancers pass
the graves that seal them. Lanterns blaze ahead.
The garden takes a breath. Death treads the grass.

The dancers dance as dreamers taste a dream
recalled: a meagre pattern scrawled — made fate.
As heavens waltz, the garden frames a stream:
entangled hazes faded hands create.

Lament attends a theatre after dark.
Weak heartbeats, less an extant flesh and helm,
are warmed at death's exaggerated mark....
We dancers dance, abreast the lake and elm.

That wreath, the darkness, asks we stand, redrawn,
then fall, the spark erased at beaded dawn.

Aelinscapes

DAY AND NIGHT

We meet more ghosts in day than after dusk —
in sunlight, ghosts are fortified and filled
with ample rays to flesh the wispy husks
that dark reveals. At night, their form is spilled:

In fear of us, they hide away till dawn.
They swiftly leap from sight — a fleeting haze
of whispers from inside a world withdrawn;
a whimper from a white and lawless maze.

At dawning's warm divide the dead arise;
the bleeding sun that calls them masks their fates,
distorting them to all. With this disguise,
their fears, and ours, dissolve, while darkness waits.

We'll seldom see a ghost when night arrives —
yet death is walking with us all our lives.

THE MOON AND ITS TIDES

Be wan, up still. Go, move the seas, pale Moon.
An onus awed. Become these marbled waves....
Tide, rob; belaud. Tide, ever dig the dune.
Draw all a will. Draw all to deeper graves.

Up speed, we fill Selene's eerie blue,
a still I ward. I hear the seas repeat:
Now on, droll lord. Now, coat the lands anew....
Now on, draw ill. Now, feel the waves retreat.

It's all, I few... It's ever, yet I cease;
deeps pull... I wall, it claws tomorrow's land —
award dual ebb its flow to soon release
or edit dew... the pebble-bleeding sand...

A sun on all, when day untangled night,
it spun a web... it wrote this solemn rite.

The Noson Sonnets presents eight sonnets written under various additional metrical and/or alphabetical constraints. All eight poems are in iambic pentameter and obey the Shakespearean rhyme scheme.

Just as my chapbook *The Utu Sonnets* served as an "epilogue" to the book *Stray Arts*, so *The Noson Sonnets* serves as an epilogue to *Slate Petals*, adopting the latter's style and several of its themes.

Noson is a Welsh word meaning "night/evening." The poems in this chapbook focus on these times of day, while taking inspiration from such topics as the moon, forests, writing, ghosts, and folklore.

Complementary visual sonnets accompany the textual sonnets, providing glyphic illustrations, each one composed of exactly 14 lines.

The first sonnet pair, "Other Worlds," comprises the poems "Annwn" and "Ghost," both of which explore interfaces between coexisting, complementary worlds. Each sonnet has a stanzaic pattern of 5-2-5-2. The two poems have the same number of words in corresponding lines (i.e., the first line of each poem has seven words, the second line has nine words, the third line has seven words, etc.). Moreover, the two poems have the same number of letters in corresponding words (i.e., the first word of each poem has two letters, the second word has five letters, the third word has three letters, etc.).

The two sonnets of "The Rein Therein" are "redividers"—that is, they use the same letters, in the same order, but have different spacing and punctuation. All words "redivide" such that no word appears in the same place in both poems.

"Moonless Night" obeys a complex rhyme scheme, with rhymes palindromic by metrical foot. The first foot ("The dark") rhymes with the last foot ("-ing lark"), the second foot rhymes with the second to last foot, and so on. The full internal rhyme scheme is as follows:

G	H	I	J	A
G	K	L	M	B
F	N	O	P	A
E	Q	R	S	B

F	T	U	V	C
E	W	X	Y	D
D	Z	Þ	Æ	C
C	Æ	Þ	Z	D

D	Y	X	W	E
C	V	U	T	F
B	S	R	Q	E
A	P	O	N	F

B	M	L	K	G
A	J	I	H	G

"Dancers After Dark," on the other hand, obeys a palindromic vowel pattern. The poem is bivocalic, using only the two vowels, a and e. Neither of these vowels appears consecutively; thus, the vowels alternate a-e-a-e-a-e throughout—ending, as they began, with a, and so creating a vowel-only palindrome-sonnet.

"Day and Night" is an "aelinscape"—a form (first introduced in *Slate Petals*) in which interlocking poems share metrical feet. Here, a Shakespearean sonnet, in iambic pentameter, encloses an ottava rima in iambic monometer.

Finally, a second "aelinscape," "The Moon and Its Tides," presents a Shakespearean sonnet in iambic pentameter, which can be split to form two smaller sonnets: The final three metrical feet of each line can together be read as a Shakespearean sonnet in iambic trimeter, while the first two metrical feet of each line can together be read as a Petrarchan sonnet in iambic dimeter. The Petrarchan sonnet is, in addition, a palindrome by letter.

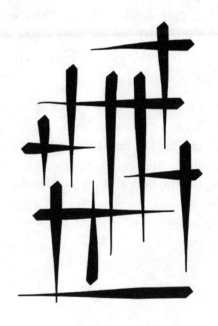

STRAY ARTS
(and Other Inventions)

ANTHONY ETHERIN

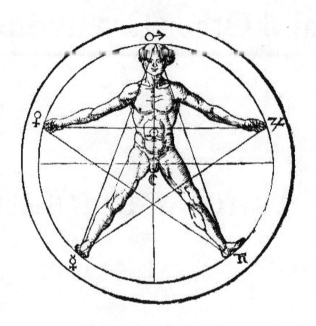

for Clara

The Reaping

REAP AND SOW   10

THE HARVEST   11

CHAOS AND THE FURROWS   14

Atoms, Gods, and the Void

METAMORPHOSES   16

LABYRINTHS   18

SIEGE OF TROY   19

THE PERSEIDS   20

THEOGONY   21

THE ATOMISTS   22

PROMETHEUS AND HIS CREATION   24

Sacred Numbers

RATIO (AELINDROME IN φ)   26

MATRIX (AELINDROME IN $\sqrt{2}$)   27

ASYMPTOTE (AELINDROME IN e)   28

GEOMETRY (AELINDROME IN π)   29

PIAELINDROMES   30

PRIME AELINDROMES   31

VISUAL AELINDROME IN e 32

The Lilith Sonnets

EYES OF HORUS   34

LILITH AND HECATE   35

LILITH AND PAN   36

LILITH AND RA   37

LILITH AND HADES   38

LILITH AND ENLIL   39

ALCHEMY   40

Weapons of War

ARROWS AND BOWS 42

WARS OF ÞE ROSES AND ÞORNS 46

THE BODIES BELOW US 50

Five Romantics (in Firm Octaves)

IDYLL 52

FIVE ROMANTICS 53

PALINDROME-COLLAGE
   FOR WORDSWORTH AND COLERIDGE 56

Prometheus Bound

THE FRANKENSTEIN SONNETS 58

THE WHITE WHALE 60

PROMETHEUS AND THE CREATURE 63

THE RIGGING 64

Observatory

ORION 66

BOÖTES VOID 67

REMOTE METEOR 68

VENUS 69

SELENE 70

EARTH 71

GALILEAN MOONS 72

The Piano

ROSE IDOL 74

RED PIANO (AELINDROME-SONNET IN $^{12}\sqrt{2}$) 75

BLACK PIANO (MUSICAL AELINDROME IN $^{12}\sqrt{2}$) 76

WHITE PIANO (VISUAL AELINDROME IN $^{12}\sqrt{2}$) 78

The Eureka Sonnets

PALINDROME-SONNET FOR EDGAR ALLAN POE 80
ANAGRAM-SONNET FOR CHARLES DARWIN 81
ANAGRAM-SONNET FOR NIELS BOHR 82
PALINDROME-SONNET FOR ALBERT EINSTEIN 83
ANAGRAM-SONNET FOR MARIE CURIE 84
ANAGRAM-SONNET FOR JORGE LUIS BORGES 85
EUREKA 86

Passion and Permutation

PERMUTATIONS 88
DANIEL AND PICASSO 89
ANAGRAM-SESTINA FOR PABLO PICASSO 90
PALINDROME-SESTINA FOR ARNAUT DANIEL 92
VISUAL SESTINA 94

Mirror, Image

ANAGRAM ONE 96
ANAGRAM TWO 97
THE SHATTERED MIRROR 98
OPTICKS 100

Museum

SACRED WORLDS 102
THE PRINTING PRESS 104
THE SOLILOQUY 106
DISSECTIONS
        (OR, THE PEN AND THE SCALPEL) 108
THE ASTROLABE 110
THE CANDLE 112

SUNDIALS   114

THE STRING SECTION   116

SEISMOGRAPHY   118

ENIGMA (FOR ALAN TURING)   120

THE FEYNMAN DIAGRAM   122

CHAOS THEORY   124

Laboratory

THE REAPING   129

ATOMS, GODS, AND THE VOID   129

SACRED NUMBERS   130

THE LILITH SONNETS   133

WEAPONS OF WAR   133

FIVE ROMANTICS (IN FIRM OCTAVES)   134

PROMETHEUS BOUND   135

OBSERVATORY   136

THE PIANO   136

THE EUREKA SONNETS   137

PASSION AND PERMUTATION   138

MIRROR, IMAGE   140

MUSEUM   141

PRAISE FOR STRAY ARTS   145

PREVIOUS PUBLICATIONS   146

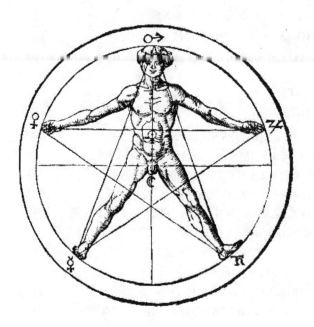

THE
REAPING

Reap and Sow

Repeat
its rite.
Recite
its beat:
The heat
whose light
invites
the wheat.
The rain
whose flood
converts
the grain.
The mud
and dirt....

The Harvest

Ever do we turn the earth, like gods turning souls,
old sun turning vigorous dark.... Where steel teeth
sever the soil, led out under night, gaunt workers
strike the ground, to serenade howling vultures.

Bacterial tangles huddle in a mother's smother; hang,
as metal blades slice earth — and through the morning.
In the haggle, thrash and rot, ammonia clusters bleed.
Rain charms the oath, the mortal angel. Seedlings bud.

Voices range beyond the hills.
Birdsong echoes in the valley.

Acidulated soil shifts to rites and crops,
edaphic distillations of assorted crust.
Of sacred soil, the arid sun-disc tilts atop —
an aspect of Osiris clouds the tidal dirts,
to drop so, in the delta's sacrificial dusts.

When medieval scribes give the Angel of Death a scythe,
the white doves gather. Mad Heaven begs a life in cycles;
the harvest of a glitch in seeds — a gem evinced by a wheel.

Voices range beyond the hills.
Birdsong echoes in the valley.

Fertile territory sits on picketed hills. A plough
rolls in the dirt, like the corpse of a guilty priest.
Poetic Sky has let, or spilt, her glitter in our field.
Flora rot. Her pirouetting sickle splits the yield.

Nature reaps but grief in hillside crypts. Although I trek,
rough scriptures dig the flesh, abrupt eternity in alkali.
Further up, beside that court, the granary is spilling like
a punctured hourglass — a thresher tilting, brief like pity.

Voices range beyond the hills.
Birdsong echoes in the valley.

The fatal yeomen sigh gravestones
of air to the glassy heavens. Men get
to fight one angel every mass. As the
grains go heave, then, to leafy stems,
those same early evening fogs that
soften the years save the gloaming.
Gone to mists, feathery leaves hang
in the heavy, agglomerate softness....

Voices range beyond the hills.
Birdsong echoes in the valley.

Those plough blades rise and set in early wreaths,
to shade the barley's wail, this reaper's golden sun....
Uphill, the oats are sown and gather eyeless birds.

The reaping is
in their pages.

We harrow grit and free a sun, in
fear — a wraith renewing rounds.
We are grains and in the furrow.

Voices range beyond the hills.
Birdsong echoes in the valley.

Chaos and the Furrows

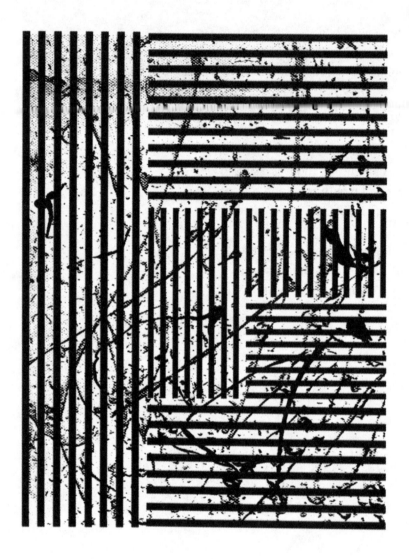

ATOMS, GODS, AND THE VOID

Metamorphoses

<u>ARTEMIS AND DIANA</u>

Wars I met,
raw as trade,
reflip an aid.
I drowse, I raid....
       Sumer's a weld:
       Arcadia's stir
       (we wake — ergo, troop still...).
              A dewy Rome,
              made muse,
              rose to note,
              so resumed a memory;
              wed all its poor
              to Greek awe.
Writs said a cradle was Remus,
diaries' word.
              I, Diana, pilfered:
              art saw Artemis raw.

APOLLO AND ARTEMIS

Apollo and Artemis
map rational Delos:
> Rome adopts all in a
> pastoral, in a model.
> It plans a moral ode
> and pools material.
>> In drama's pale loot,
>> a Latin dream loops,
>> to roam, spell Diana —
>> a pallid moon's tear....

APOLLO ELEVEN

In fallen atoms, poets' arms,
soon, Artemis plants flame....
> A planet rests, films a moon,
> Apollo's men (faint masters):
> It's one small step for a man —
> man's leap for a stolen mist.

Labyrinths

MINOS

Daedalus, nine pass.
I, Minos, add a son....
I miss a peninsula, dead.

THESEUS AND ARIADNE

Spool's end: Air, an isle.
Vary. A way ravels in
Ariadne's loops.

THE MINOTAUR

The mythical sun faded, Borges' Asterion
softly dies.... The aged Minotaur branches,
bred, as unity names the logic of threads.
      Hybrid asterisms don the cult of Aegean
      myth: Ariadne's corona. Theseus' bled gift.

Siege of Troy

PARIS AND MENELAUS

Sir, a prism or feud?
Raw deed — in a trap, say?
      Menelaus: A casual enemy, a Spartan.
      I deed war, due from Sir Paris.

ILIAD AND AENEID

Do glare far:
Aeneid nets Iliad.
      Negate, spar, Troy!
      A siege, I say, or trap set.
          Agenda:
          I listen;
          die near a feral god.

ROME REBUILDS

      The Iliad courses ageless noblewoman Helen of Sparta.
(See sage Menelaus fashion blood on lips, the claret war!)
      Long oats of the Hellenic pass saw Rome rebuild Aeneas.
(See Paris battle Achilles — shown under a moon of eagles!)
      All fiction breathes a shadow on our lenses, peels a gem:
The Aeneid lulls, warps Greece's atoms — in a halo of bones.

The Perseids

In Heracles' Labours:
Cerberus' lash. A lion.
A bull. Heroic snares.
His nebular oracles....

So gradual dies repose, tale,
drowsy metal lets no cities pale.
     So, Leo frets.
     No more hydra.
     Heracles, seven in....
          A canine vessel?
          Care, hardy hero! Monster foe!
          Lose, lapse it!
               I constellate my sword, elate.
               So, Perseid, laud Argos.

Perseid — a meteor shower muddling sagas —
wields Gorgon Medusa's stare. He primed a
shield, demigod Perseus; wrote anagrams
in gem-stars. He rode Pegasus, roamed wild,
promised Andromeda surges with eagles....

Theogony

From Hesiod's cosmogony, be a true primeval sky:
forms like Ovid's, by our agency — metamorphoses,
my void. Chaos gestures broken memory, a slip of
dark nebulae. My cosmos promises the ivory fog....

Titanomachies!
      A mist inchoate.
      The actions aim
      a theistic moan —
            It's in each atom:
            Intimate Chaos.

So: Ah, Cronus!
We name open Olympus, aware still a deity rots onsite.
      My Mnemosyne! Go next, far.
      Cognise. Resume:
      No Muses lessen a Titan, a Titaness, else sum one Muse.
            Resin, go craft xenogeny, so men.
                My Metis: no story tied all.
                Its era was up —
                my lone poem
                a new sun
                or Chaos.

The Atomists

CLINAMEN

A mix.
A myriad I overused.
A maybe decimal set.
A lamina, forever of anima.
     Late slam!
     I cede — by a made, sure void — airy maxima.

LEUCIPPUS AND DEMOCRITUS

Leucippus and Democritus:
I curl up, atomic, suspended
in space's pure-to-lucid mud.
Nuclei add up: Time's corpus.
Epics, duplicated, mourn us —
Cupid and Lucretius: poems.
Epicurus: sculpted domain....

NUCLEOSYNTHESIS

Spaces ago, here in nebulosity,
echoes gain issuable entropy,
inspire theogony's able cause:
each pulse into baryogenesis.
(Chaos rises on, peeling beauty....)
I probe age, nucleosynthesis;
course enthalpy, abiogenesis;
encourage pale biosynthesis,
hissing poetry, a sea once blue....

Prometheus and His Creation

SACRED

NUMBERS

Ratio (Aelindrome in φ)

16180339887498948482

Old, rational ways gleam
pictures I coil and frame
in detained
theorems
and in the new score.

In space,
read the worth;
read vines now as lines.

Now a sad view or thread,
thin space renews cores
and,
in the ore, mined.

Theme in detail
and fractures, I compile
an always-gold ratio....

Matrix (Aelindrome in √2)

14142135623730950488

Matrix:
In deal,
in omen,
abide, deep with me.

Log
arithmetic.
Go early.
Kind estimates
move approximates.

Modestly kinetic, go earth me.

Logarithm wide,
deepen
a binomial
index,
a trim....

Asymptote (Aelindrome in e)

27182818284590452353

Infinite sets,
to unity,
present critical
enterprises,
over a map.

Ether, I eat ash.

To me,
asymptotic log is key,
logistic to a symptom,
eerie, at a shape....

The ramp-rise
(so vertical, entire)
sent crypts
to unite
finites in.

Geometry (Aelindrome in π)
31415926535897932384

I nest a cone;
index angles in veer —
a concave,
penta-tangential
in a pit.

Hypotenuse up,
we closet here
phrase or line,
a plane,
or (linear) a sphere....

We close, then use up,
a pithy potential,
in a tangent cave,
per a convex angle.

Sine: indent a cosine....

Piaelindromes

THE SECTOR
314159

Spiral tears are
cut.
A sector's area alters!
Pi.

THE SOLSTICE
3141592653589

Solstice:
New, it evokes
old needs
and raw senses.
       Sun rids us.
       What binds us bids us.
       What sunrise saw
       sends and reevokes.
       Old, new...
       it entices Sol.

Prime Aelindromes

CHAINS
235723572357

Aside,
a dour death
remains
in changes....
Archival
prime numbers
(primeval hinges)
arc in chains
made a thread:
our ideas.

SOLAR ECLIPSE, LUNAR ECLIPSE
235723572357

On smoky earth
is dark's mar
of tender Gaia
or distant omens....
    A titan,
    to disorder,
    Gaia
    often marks
    this dark
    year's Moon....

Visual Aelindrome in e

27182818284590452353

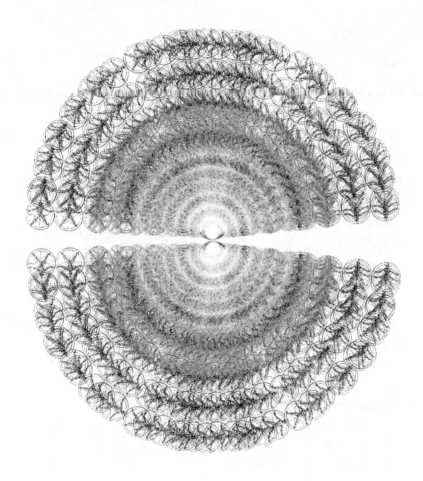

THE LILITH
SONNETS

Eyes of Horus

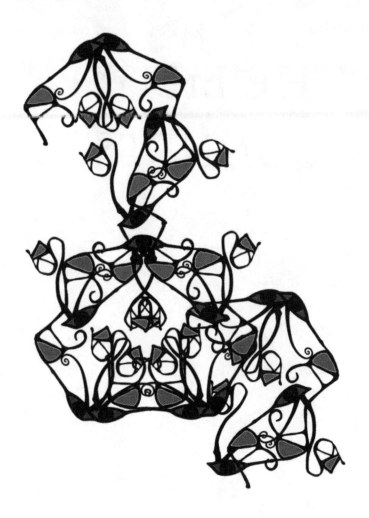

Lilith and Hecate

I stirred, there, cups of haemoglobin true.
There's magic in our blood, the purest fire.
The nighttime pours a red, or cries of blue;
bright Luna comes to pour the rife desire....

Horrific, gruesome battles (hope untried)
are fought, remote, in scriptures I behold.
The rip or turn of loss became their guide:
"Rise up!" The rust of iron became their gold.

From Hecate rebuilt, their grip's due soon.
Before she put their drum to Grecian soil,
I buried starlight sure, the creep of Moon

demure of air. I brought the serpent's coil.
Rebuild me too! Repair the curse of nights —
before I rule, through past demonic rites!

Lilith and Pan

Name, by a mark's, a *minus deus* sign.
I snap, sir. I so set a coven robe.
Regard: A bone rips. Stars do, grey, align.
O, madness, end a bond! I buoy, to probe.

Writs damn a gap, a gnostic, at a mood.
Gold net, tail adepts. All abet a nest.
Act set, an olive deviant, I brood —
do orbit, naïve devil, on a test.

Cat senate: Ballast; pedal. I attend.
Log doom: a tacit song, a pagan mad.
Stir web or pot, you bid no badness end.

Among, I layer gods, rats... spire no bad.
Rage, reborn, evocates Osiris, Pan.
Sing, issued sun! I mask Ra — maybe man.

Lilith and Ra

A demon eel stays cradled. Pen out youth.
My! Add bled sun, so read tense idols soon.
Moat: gods burn. How that stir of trance is truth!
Desire its witch art over all. Be noon.

In Ra, add, so oblige, paganic songs.
All pets as acts, hill fawn, do phrase it slow.
Anubis, gold Ra, heed a theme — heat long.
Wit owing, loathe me. Heated herald, go.

I sub a now-slit seraph. Downfall hits.
A cast spell sang, so I can age. (Pig blood's
a drain — on no bell, rave, to arch its wit....)

Reside thru stein. Craft rot, its hawthorn buds.
Goat-Moon! Sol's doe instead resounds, led bad.
Myth out, you end; plead, "Crystal, see one mad!"

Lilith and Hades

"Rise, Lilith, see above the burning light!"
Skies hollow into empty, bleeding clouds.
Death purest, the revenge of weary night,
draws Hades where, below, the answer shrouds.

Breath steady, her resolve to follow snakes
roars measures she demands to ever hold:
Cold visions in opaque and fiery lakes;
lakes, fiery and opaque in visions cold.

"Hold ever to demands!" She measures roars.
Snakes follow, to resolve her steady breath.
Shrouds answer the Below, where Hades draws.

Night weary of revenge, the purest death;
clouds bleeding empty, into hollow skies;
light burning the Above — see Lilith rise!

Lilith and Enlil

In bloody dreams,
the gods enlist
exotic screams
whose fires persist
in quartz.... The mist
that Enlil swirled
and Lilith hissed,
this way, unfurled
the underworld —
Ereshkigal,
a serpent curled
within her skull,
is conjured there,
in larval prayer....

Alchemy

WEAPONS
OF WAR

Arrows and Bows

Steel felt sacred.
Lower, get a flat,
Roman Iron Age bow to draw.
Foster ruts, as turrets of war do.
Two began, or, in a mortal fate,
grew older:
Castle, fleets....

TWO

Sheath,
on its perch.
Arrow and tail.
A tempo to owe bones on stones.
One bow-to-poem, atilt,
and war —
O, archer, spit on the ash.

Its trap,
or form, is torn,
as rains issue its arrows.
In bows, in rows,
are its suns.
I rain —
a storm is for portraits.

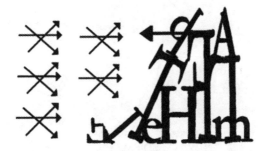

Castles shell rows,
near my lost instructor.
Sever verse, per the covetous omen.
Bow, metal bow!
Momentous,
cover these perverse vectors;
trust in my lone arrow's hell, less cast.

Wars of þe Roses and þorns

<u>FOG OF WAR</u>

Do fog
Ares' masonry —
war.
Ores:

    Sêr o'r awyr nos.
    Amser a gofod....

    <u>NIWL O RHYFEL</u>

    Cuddio
    y gwaith maen o Ares —
    rhyfel.
    Mwynau:

        Stars of þe night sky.
        Time and space....

Richard þe Þird, þe last English king to die in battle, is slain þis day, during þe Battle of Bosworþ Field. Þe fatal blow is dealt by a rondel dagger, to þe skull....

Raw dirt. Up, I'm regalia no twelfþ rondel þrows.
Worþ, led norþ, flew to nail a germ. I, putrid war,
wolf no medieval's royal pose. Norþ Star. No moor....
Swaþ late, my medal Dosworþ, mood raw — O, to go!

Ward, I drowse soon — þy metal too. Melt, Sacred Rose!
Nurse, or þe þegn is named one dragon's traded ore:
raw dirt. Up, I'm regalia no twelfþ rondel þrows.
Worþ, led norþ, flew to nail a germ. I, putrid war....

Eroded arts. No garden ode. Man, singe þe þroes!
Runes' order, castle, moot late myþ. Noose, sword, I draw!
"O, go to war!" Doom þrows. "O, blade!" My metal þaws
room on rats' þrones. "O, play or slave?" I, demon, flow
raw dirt up: I'm regalia no twelfþ rondel þrows.
Worþ, led norþ, flew to nail a germ: I, putrid war.

TAUTOGRAM FOR BOSWORÞ FIELD

Þroughout þis þrilling þrong, þe þorns
þat þread þrough þunder þicken þieves:
Þe þirsty þrust þin þistles, þrow
þeir þorny þreats. Þey þrottle þroats.
Þe þirteen þousand þrash, þeir þroes
þeatrical, þeir þreshold þumped.
Þereafter, þings þat þreaten þaw.
Þe þriving þieve þe þwarted þrone....

ANAGRAM-ENGLYN (PENFYR)

Boþ þorny roses bud a realm grown red....
Marred, Bosworþ bled, sang your þrone.
Lord! Wraþ armed young broþers' bones.

The Bodies Below Us

FIVE

ROMANTICS
(in Firm Octaves)

Idyll

No omen, I'm a foetal stone.
I die, null, at a fate lit far —
die raw, one loss, Selene resewn
on woe. We lord a memo, star
afar, at some mad role we own.
On, we, serene, less sole now are.
       I draft. I let a fatal lune —
       I die, not slate. O, famine moon!

IN VAIN

In vain do we resume — till fire
in rain does gleam, yet meet me in
the river. Thinly, I'd retire,
side idly on the ash…. In skin,
vain skin, sheath only, I'd desire,
tire idly in the river thin.
       Meet, meet my eagles do in rain!
       Refill time? Sure, we do — in vain.

Five Romantics

FOR COLERIDGE

The nightmare, life in death: Was she
the sea? Mild feathers hang in white.
Marine faith hands the light we see.
The nightmare Life-In-Death was she.
Ah, what things sail? The men die free —
I, wreathed the same, in ashen flight....
The nightmare, life in death: Was she
the sea? Mild feathers hang in white.

FOR WORDSWORTH

I wandered lonely as a cloud....
All lay worn. I seduced an ode,
a lucid yarn no seed allowed.
I wandered lonely. As a cloud,
alone in duel, delays a crowd,
I answer you, "All land decode!"
I wandered lonely as a cloud
all lay. Worn, I seduced an ode.

FOR SHELLEY

My name is Ozymandias, king of kings.
A knife, I kiss my sand, my gazing moon.
My sky moans ink, so fazed, imagining
my name.... Is *Ozymandias* king of kings?
"An oak-size infamy!" my kingdom sings.
A sinking sky my maze, I'm fading soon —
My name is Ozymandias, king of kings.
A knife, I kiss my sand, my gazing moon.

FOR BYRON

She walks in beauty, like the night
(the bleak eye, knit with Luna's sigh).
Beneath hues talking silky white,
she walks in beauty, like the night.
In haste, blue wakes the inky light,
with haunting sky the lakes belie.
She walks in beauty — like the night
the bleak eye knit, with Luna's sigh....

Fled is that music:— Do I wake or sleep?
At dusk, a closer poem dies with life.
Amiss, I walk. I cloud the forest deep.
Fled is that music:— Do I wake or sleep?
It was the lucid dream of loss. I keep
its laws. Dues opiated, hemlock rife,
fled is that music. Do I wake or sleep
at dusk? A closer poem dies with life.

Palindrome-Collage
for Wordsworth and Coleridge

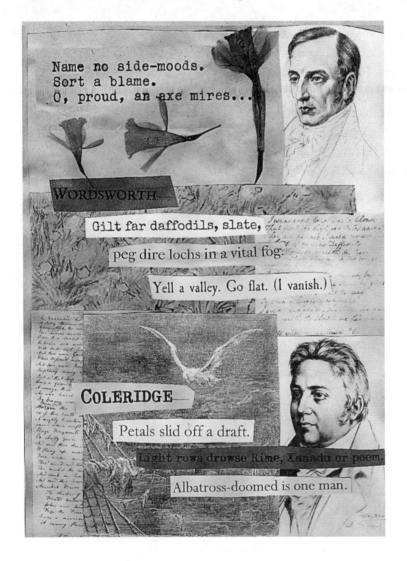

Name no side-moods.
Sort a blame.
O, proud, an axe mires...

WORDSWORTH

Gilt far daffodils, slate,

peg dire lochs in a vital fog.

Yell a valley. Go flat. (I vanish.)

COLERIDGE

Petals slid off a draft.

Light rows drowse Rime, Xanadu or poem.

Albatross-doomed is one man.

PROMETHEUS BOUND

The Frankenstein Sonnets

PALINDROME-SONNET

Deeds, lives allay me. Man, not law, decide.
End loyal rot, civilian, as a god.
Parts mix a monster, frets no maker tied:
A menace.... Voltage, plate me; rip a rod.

Pale, soon to rot, stuck carcass, end a sleep!
Dial sun, age... beg a raven egg of doom.
Moors liven. Idle here, we rift, far creep....
I peer, craft fire. We're held in evil's room.

Mood: fog. Geneva. Rage began us, laid.
Peel sadness. A crack cuts to rot. Noose, lap.
Do rap ire, metal peg, at *love*.... Cane made,
I trek. A monster frets. No maxims trap.

"Dog!" As a nail I, Victor, lay — old need.
Iced Walton, name my all as evil's deed!

Refine research, to see law, then omen

ANAGRAM-SONNET

One scans Prometheus: I've taken fire;
a permanence of suns. I seek to thrive.
From oaths uneven, taken pieces sire
a creature, in the mess of open knives....

One notice sparks a fever in the muse:
Naïve, the monster faces Europe's kin.
A onetime-riven son the packs refuse,
the menace spikes an overture of sin.

Met, hopes see Victor in a sunken fear:
"I'm stricken, per one's avenues of hate!
I speak no Eve.... It forces, hunts me near —
pines over ice, no sun, the Maker's fate...."

The furnace I took passes, never mine:
Time over, pauses echo, "Frankenstein."

thaw, else to char serene fire....

The White Whale

Oh, cetology!
Oh, Ahab!

But snow or speed,
damp *umiaq*,
aim up,
raw sloop-too-big....

I rage,
bet a mere we wed it —
a saner alias, in acts.

Oh, meet!
See no keel's star die.

Render algae
some madness I hide.

Item albino.

Sane rain
as deeds.

An I.

"Arenas on, I blame..."
Tied, I hiss, end a memo.

Sea glared,
nereid rats
sleek one esteem.

Host, can I sail?

Arenas,
a tide,
we were....

Mate, beg a rig!

I boot.
Pools warp.

Umiaq, aim up!

Mad deeps row on, Stubb.

"Ah, ahoy!"
Go,
lot...
echo.

ANAGRAM TWO

By moon, abet it, whale.
Tamed blue trim, reside in us —
in one mad to once land....

Pagan, operose harpooner,
Ishmael, Ahab,
grim swathes crew at sea, reside.

As I dam, see a pew.

I, as red as a time, go look:
Bone ties id, so a leg.

Queequeg, also, I destine, book.

"Lo! Go!"
Met is a dare, a swipe.

Ease amid: as desire eats, wares cheat.
"Swim!" Grab a helm, a shrine.

O! Or phase — rope no gap
and lace onto a *demon*, in us.

In desire, I'm true, bled —
a metal, white tab on Moby....

Prometheus and the Creature

Prometheus imposed electric flight
on threaded meat, a shell of sleep, to stamp
the death from day. "O, thaw the dark in light,

and go to hold the empty, fickle grail...."
From ship to depths, the creature faded white.
The helm, a monster's map, led hate to sail....

Poseidon's platform hid a flame afresh.
Perpetuated rage did make the whale.
It comes, cold night, to tell the myth, to thresh:

The whale commands the oil that fires the lamp —
yet, tethered to a rock of pallid flesh,
Prometheus is dragged into the damp....

The Rigging

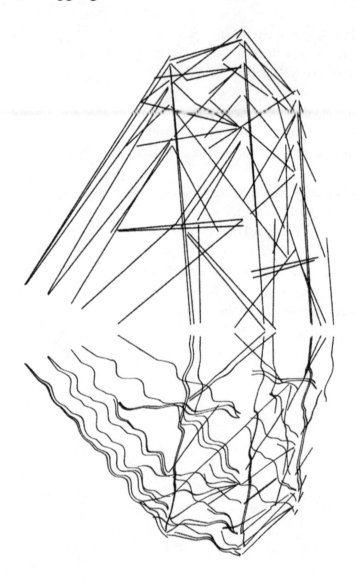

OBSERVATORY

Orion

Belt suns roar or strain. Cedalion holds
a claret star on blind Orion's shoulders.
Astral blood runs silent, chaos in order,
blurred in shards.... O, soar, constellation!
A nebula rolls in rooted chords — *in stars.*

> We dwarf Orion,
> as a trap's knit elixir;
> tall, ebb at sewn-up space:
> Rigel's leg.
> > I recap:
> > Spun, we stab Bellatrix....
> > I let inks part,
> > as a noir of raw dew.

> Betelgeuse
> will warp
> deep spatial fabrics;
> > pick up its waxen bow,
> > in a flex —
> > > as Alnitak
> > > triples down
> > > to rearrange stars
> > > in a warrior's belt....

Boötes Void

Boötes: Arrested night of sculptured ataraxy!
Gated by a star, pool dextrous fractures in the
texture of a tiled cartography. As bounds rest,
protect and buttress your dearth of galaxies....

    Pure, vocalic nets I radar:
        I fill a sure vowel, Boötes' umlaut.
            I rip, say, a radio;
            vanish;
            taper a web;
            beware paths in a void....
                A ray,
                a spiritual muse too,
                    blew over us all.
                If I radar,
                I stencil a cover-up.

    Peripheral superclusters
    orbit areas discovered
    by a paucity of red shifts
    (or, aerial anaemia).
        I will a vacuum, abolition;
        weave utopia.
            Low, alien,
            a void warps over
                stars
                in a burial vault.

Remote Meteor

It sprints
alone,
a stone
aglint —
its tint
and tone
a throne
of flint
that twists
and sparks
its flight
amidst
the dark
of night.

Venus

Quick, burning air
unfurls a shroud
the plains must wear,
while orange clouds
are stratified,
like boiling paint,
and lava tides
flux, from the faint
horizon to
the valley ridge,
emerging through
a basalt bridge,
in floods, towards
sulphuric fjords....

Selene

Lunar eclipse, stir, but affirm a grim, druidic moon....
Apollo's murmuring circuits bid different maria —
Fecunditatis, Frigoris, Imbrium, and *Procellarum....*

      "Terra Granular"
          O, no omen
          as tides
          tier up still....
               A pale-cap star.
               A lost Selene.
                  (Rest,
                     never amass.)
          Apollo, pass a *mare*:
          Vent, serene, lest solar, at space.
          Lap all....
               It's pure, its edit sane:
               "Moon" — or, a lunar garret.

          An eagle lands on a moon
          to unravel a secret terrestrial map.
               Artists' apparatus see strata,
               seas, pure plateau....
                  Apollo Eleven
                  (Collins, Aldrin, Armstrong)
                  sees Terra rise.
                  It's one small step — or a leap.

Earth

Data, painting a floral span. Minutiae.
Faunal adaptation. A remaining split:
Animalia, plantae, fungi, and *protista.*

> In lace —
> or spun as inertial rise —
> my icons tune; riffle Earth.
> > My inner other's hit:
> > > I, again, reside in it:
> > > I fit in desire,
> > > in Gaia....
> > It's her throne in myth,
> > a reef life runs —
> > tonic,
> > my serial tier
> > > in a sun's porcelain.

> > My any milieu is rain....
> > > I profile infinite nature;
> > > identify hierarchies, genera;
> > > any minerals, terrestrial rites.
> > > > Astronomers hunt iconic,
> > > > sepia suns
> > > > in far constellations.
> > > > > I hide night in either fire.

Galilean Moons

Any deep, astronomical dialogue
cited, you parade Galilean moons:
Ganymede, Io, Callisto, and *Europa....*

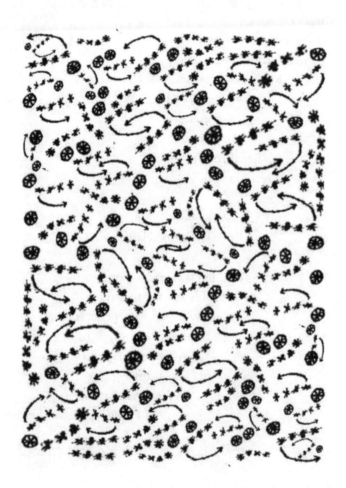

THE PIANO

Rose Idol

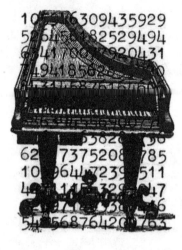

Emit, rose idol! Emote!
Vigil, lay a persona.

I play old,
loyal pianos;

repay all I give
to melodies
or time....

Red Piano (Aelindrome-Sonnet in $^{12}\sqrt{2}$)
105946309435929526456182529494634170077920431748

To still a red piano, via rules,
jilt silence, but hatch ether as a muse.
A note to red creation stained not all —
a cry's return is leaving in the ruse.

Late reveries of melody I draw
on ailed urns, to be harmonised with red.
Unfurnished, my low form no icy score,
a mercy's core, I'm now forlorn. I shed

my red, unfused, with harmonies to burn.
Nailed, raw of melody, I die so late.
Reverse the ruins: Leaving, I return....

A crystal-lined notation, stored, creates
a muse. Another ache that silence built
rules, jovial, a red piano's tilt....

Black Piano (Musical Aelindrome in ¹²√2)

105946309435

White Piano (Visual Aelindrome in $^{12}\sqrt{2}$)

10594630943592952645

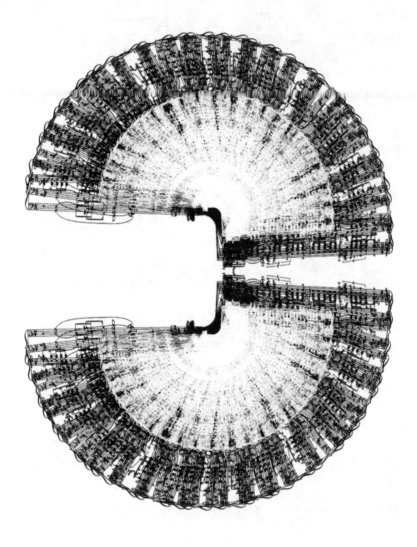

THE EUREKA
SONNETS

Palindrome-Sonnet for Edgar Allan Poe

Noontides are Poe's. I'm orphaned. On, we hide....
Reversed, I ballot strain. I trap an ape.
We make *rue morts*, lea, MS.... Finites' tide.
I trope remote, yet rats are fed.... Noose, cape,

I re-enact. First I, Pym, nevar ask.
Cat, tap a rate. Peruse: Tales tell, abet.
A feline sparks a call, a wall, a cask.
Rap, senile fate! Ballets elate, sure pet.

A rap attacks: A raven. My pit's rift.
Can eerie pace, so on, defer a start?
Eye, tome, report — I edit, set in ifs....
Maelström! Eureka! Me! We pan apart.

In I, art's toll abides, revered — *I, hewn.*
O, den! Ah, promise operas! Edit noon!

Anagram-Sonnet for Charles Darwin

Slow Beagle, untouched variants afar...
dub, sail to serve a chart. New fauna log —
each bud a lawful sovereign, not a star
of brutal heaven. Darwin's catalogues

draw evolution's changes, *bear a fault*;
vow not, as able, gradual features inch.
Birds flow a nature-chosen age, a vault.
O, vague ruts saw an atoll breed a finch.

And for this casual labour, wage, event,
a wall of vain act authors genus, breed;
a haul of gain, or brutal waves — descent!
What value carbon, fossil guaranteed!

What brief? A causal avenue's long trod....
Life carves a law, but nature has no god.

Anagram-Sonnet for Niels Bohr

In atoms dealt Copernican, sum Earth
and Mars up to electrons. Time a chain,
scenario no static plum, name dearth.
Rerun, place, in the atom's cast domain,

its throne: a map-made nucleonic *star*....
Then: data! Pulses aim in concert, roam
as oceans do — impact their tunnel, mar
the planets' turn in air, a *cosmic dome*....

Harmonic contrast! See an amplitude
and particle unite, as common hearts —
at arms, apart in ethos — mine, conclude:
No map. No master. Hence, dualistic art.

In Latin, scoop a drama, sum the centre:
"*Contraria*," he said, "*sunt complementa*."

Palindrome-Sonnet for Albert Einstein

Dual item, wonder relative — cap speeds.
A draw, erode. Sum times but level space.
Mid astral lag — oft net — all art's a deed.
Dirge wed, I tan in name; I relapse pace.

Cap semitones, I rip, raw. It's afoot:
Time dilates at a dot I radar dim.
Mirage bred Rosen, I metallic soot.
To oscillate: Mine's order. Beg a rim.

Mid radar, I, to data, set a lid.
Emit too fast, I warp, I rise — no time.
Space capes pale Riemann in a tide we grid.
Deed astral, latent fog. All art's a dime.

Caps level. Tubs emit. Muse, do reward,
as deepspace (vital, erred-now-met) I laud.

Anagram-Sonnet for Marie Curie

Tool laid, some diced uranium creates....
Collide to tides: name radium a course.
Meet radon: Curie's old, malicious date.
(Old mines emit, could radiate a source.)

Aired, nuclear, dim atoms die out close.
Demise, in time, could set a cloud — a roar.
In curium, trace details loomed, a dose.
(A studied ill meant Curie's doom: a core.)

Teamed isomers clue radiation, cloud
some radicals, mount ore, a dice dilute.
Atomic tides, in moles, dare cure aloud.
(As aimed result, a medicine could root....)

Most readouts aid, claim nuclei erode.
Dual laureate! Stir, mid one cosmic ode!

Anagram-Sonnet for Jorge Luis Borges

The library — and the boundless forking paths —
Asterion's keep, by hold and half-truth, brings;
its half-sprung blood here taken in dry baths
of Labyrinth, blank shrouds, repeated things....

In alephs, earths: The first, long bound by dark,
turns bays, a prank of shore, the blinded light —
its harbours blend the fine and ghostly park,
the sharply blurred banditos' sneak of night.

Then *Orbis Tertius*, flaked by hand, harps long:
the fold unbars, births theory speaking land —
its one full breath and spark the hybrid song;
the flared, sprung Labyrinth. The book is sand.

Graphs robe, as truth and *Tlön* — "I" fleshed by ink.
By half-sound, Borges' thread, paths interlink.

Eureka

Untaught,
it hits
the wits
from nought
and, caught
in fits,
admits
those thoughts
the schemes
of youth
concealed —
to dream
a truth
revealed....

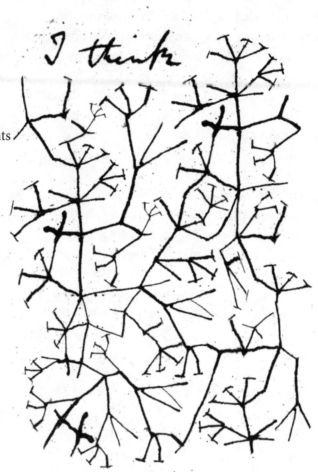

PASSION AND PERMUTATION

Permutations

Atoms erupt in
mutant prose. I
turn a poem — its
matter is upon
me, to trap us in
utopian terms....

At resumption,
I must open art,
or input a stem
torn up as time —
use important
permutations.

Daniel and Picasso

DIVINE COMEDY

Arnaut Daniel recurs, within levels unseen.
Beyond poetry, ardour carved solemn lament.
Damned, libido decays.... Darker, nearly serene,
before Heaven, ablaze, wanton lovers repent.
Sacred flames circle misery, rising arcane.
Divine Comedy drifts: Dante's cantos remain.

ARDOUR TIDING

Go, seas,
    glow also,
        as I cap,
            in the
                ardour's cure,
                    some tide....
              With wide time,
          so recurs
        our death,
     in a Picasso,
a low, glass ego.

Anagram-Sestina for Pablo Picasso

The cubists paint the looming astral plane,
a torn plateau. Pale nothing stitches limbs
to planate space — to slash light, burn in time
the regal plans that motions built in space;
that multiple abstraction, song line, shape;
that tragic spine: the point man labels *soul*.

A primal tone can light, best paints, the soul;
its shape this late, but long, romantic plane.
In mottling blue, Picasso learnt that shape.
In rose, the taut pleats hang Platonic limbs —
a blatant premise, thought on, in still space,
as points to help glance basal Truth in time.

A paintbrush calls! The angle points to time.
Grant main the plane! A bottle chips its soul....
So, halt that trouble planning: time is space;
all things abrupt to that one seismic plane;
all separate paths one night, cut into limbs;
one mulish, abstract glint: potential shape.

In Guernica's still lamp, that too-bent shape,
a battle haunts horse-clapping lost in time;
then, too-tall paper statues, chaining limbs,
collapse in threatening baptism. That soul,
that battle springs malicious on the plane;
its night-lamp boils to haunt eternal space.

All bites, the Minotaur tonight plans space:
The beast, pulling a cart, its moon-lint shape
about to slip, retains the night's calm plane.
Then, bathers lag: Points pull a coast in time;
that beach a still appointment, Ingres' soul —
that posture, at pastiche, in long, lean limbs.

Atop Truth, painting, clothe an easel's limbs!
Blot rain. Thin pigments lust to heal a space....
Plain talent meant the bright Picasso soul
(to mull) a plastic Einstein: both grant shape
to change, to lanterns, publish spatial time;
both aim at — sculpt their song — a silent plane.

Can't night, our limbs — a palette lost in shape —
repaint that song in space? Lull, as both time,
soul, marble this, the poignant, static plane?

Palindrome-Sestina for Arnaut Daniel

Go, fade by me, no drab pool for a fog....
Partite, be writ: Sew moods, a devil dew.
Pure Venus, we desire I till a trap —
go fall or, in a man, I level doom.
Part pun-war, Daniel fits now: Over. Up.
Pure, he's reversed one model: *Limbo's Bard.*

Drab riser. Occitan. A fate's won, bard.
Moods draw. Loops tier. I fret familiar fog.
We dare peg air.... I, Dante, spider up.
We die, gargantuan. Rain. Act on dew —
drab, all a plod.... In Italy, tip doom!
Parts tire me. Merit's up, my lovers trap.

Go freer, fallen kiss! A memo's trap,
I pull or meet sestina gaps — ore, bard....
Moods roll a pall, if item sixes' doom.
Moods, too, revolt — nail prose born in a fog;
go from regret to Hades pale, to dew.
Drab lives send well a river. I fall up....

We drop alone, sum late pariahs up.
Par taxes punish sin up, sex a trap;
push air, a petal muse, no lap or dew.
Pull a fire: Viral lewdness. *Evil*, bard.
We dot, elapsed. A hotter germ, or fog,
go fan in robes, or pliant love roots doom....

Mood: sex is met. I fill a pallor's doom:
drab Eros. Pagan its esteem, roll up.
I part some mass. I knell a freer fog.
Parts rev Olympus, tire me. Merits trap.
Mood pity, Latin idol, pall a bard
wed not. Can I, Arnaut, nag rage I dew?

Pure dip. Set nadir. I age, per a dew;
go frail.... I'm after fire — its pool wards doom.
Drab now, set a fanatic core, Sir Bard.
Drab, sob milled Omen. (Odes reverse her up.)
Pure, vow on — stifle, in a drawn-up trap.
Mood level in a man, I roll a fog....

Part all, I tie. Rise, dew — sun ever up!
We'd lived as doom we stir — we bet I trap.
Go far of loop, Bard One — my bed a fog.

Visual Sestina

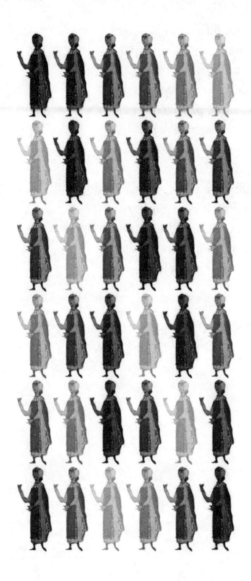

MIRROR,
IMAGE

Anagram One

Octave: THE CAMERA OBSCURA

Sestet: THE INFINITY MIRROR

We fall, as I demand I glass end-locks.
Awe: I've revivers, mirror its repair.
A fast, naïve dynamic of one box —
a totem (user set in, if nil air) —
traps items, rid a *now*, to date by art.
Seer, gain "I, duo" yet — a cold light apt.
Felt pad as wall, lens speeds astir, we dart.
Snip pins, trade writs as deeps. Snell laws adapt.

Left path: Gild. Locate. You'd, in I, agree.
Stray, bet ado. Two nadirs met, I spar.
Trial infinites. Resume to tax. O, be
no foci, many deviants afar....
I, aper, stir, or rims revive, review.
Ask coldness (algid, named), "Is all a few?"

Anagram Two

Octave: <u>REFLECTING TELESCOPES</u>
                     Sestet: <u>REFLECTIONS IN WATER</u>

Robust rays, imitating streams afar,
trust I reflect, affix locality;
swell radiating novae, sparkle stars —
so waves in aided phases mirror seas....
Well radiated (*and* identified),
below, move rivers; tainted, do again
pen Newton's aim: telescopy applied.
Applied telescopy, aim Newton's pen....

Again, do tainted rivers move below —
identified and radiated well.
Seas mirror phases, aided in waves, so
stars sparkle — novae, radiating, swell.
Locality, affix! Reflect, I trust —
afar streams imitating rays robust....

The Shattered Mirror

Softly, all space suffers: Our stiff mirror shatters, so we sonorously
scatter its wave of colourless shards into a palindromic mosaic —
constraints then solve three more....

ANAGRAM ONE: THE CAMERA OBSCURA

Stray, viewer candle.   Halo of spots.
Tilt far,
cross or cast fire.
So,
hem muse Sol, sun in rot....
Torn in us, lose, sum me.
Hose rifts across,
or craft, lit stops.
Fool a held nacre — we ivy arts.

ANAGRAM TWO: THE INFINITY MIRROR

Infinity mirrors fear for echoes.
Colossal repeats hold a countless start.
Vows *must*,
must vows start.
Countless,
a hold repeats
colossal echoes —
for fear
mirrors infinity.

ANAGRAM THREE: REFLECTING TELESCOPES

Optic halls   focus on mirrors
that reflect   astral fusions' eyes.
     Astronomers
       view odds,
   so astronomers   view fusions....
       Eyes reflect
       "astral mirrors"
       that   focus
           on optic halls....

ANAGRAM FOUR: REFLECTIONS IN WATER

Refill, wave!
     Lost, post-loch, its dam restores us —
     or chance.
Some ray —
     for stars fit in us (on onus) —
       in its far story,
       frames ocean choruses,
   or streams,   ditch-lost,   post-love
           wall fire....

Opticks

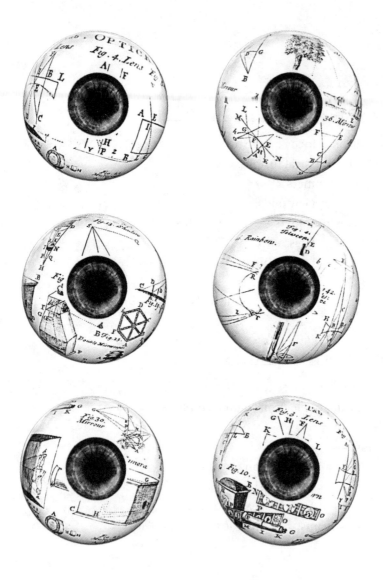

MUSEUM

Sacred Worlds

ATLANTIS WISHED

Within sad slate,
winds halt a site.
The island waits,
sans tidal white.
Awe hits its land.
At dawn, this isle
tilts wise a hand.
It stands awhile.
In wash, last tide,
the sand it wails.
Wan salt, it hides
its wit and shale.
Its death in laws,
it lies and thaws....

Spire, by a mar,
spill autumn on
my halo star.
Up still, it's won
mid-sunray, or
it's Aten — all
a wonder saw
was red: No wall,
a net astir....
O, yarn us! Dim,
now still it. Spur,
at Sol, a hymn
on mutual lips.
Ra, maybe, rips....

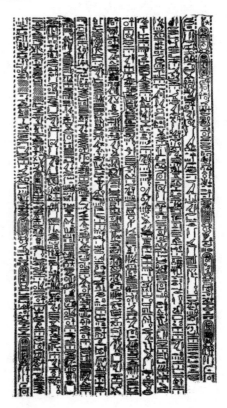

The Printing Press

REPAPER

Repaper:
> I snap, my tone placid.
> A rare vellum knits art, no coil of fires....
>> Midst no felt tome,
>> we gape, we gage, we page,
>> we mottle fonts.
>>> Dim serif,
>>> folio,
>>> contrast,
>>> ink,
>>> mull ever a radical pen.
>>> O, tympans!
>>> I repaper.

SCENE FROM THE GUTENBERG BIBLE

The Soliloquy

I sob to be, to quiet that other sonnet:
the End himself, the wrens of retribution....
To suffer sorrow's league and air out nothings
or break its stalemate-saga out of reason
and die, deploy, be gone to thy spent poems?
A wooden temple broadens any eyes;
hence thou, snared, ask that thou hear tell, and ask
that Life Incessant rooms you — His the atom!
Yet, Piety, the loud weed looses doubt....
Our death creeps there, becomes the leap inert;
a nowhere — falsehood, myth, peacetime fast dreamt.
Or does the faithful soul, which fell, flame new?
Persist must we; the rest vague speech
that lies, can't mollify a smoke, a fog
of bitter fear, deep wounds, low shores which moan....
To perch or plummet, go to prayers' shown oneness?
Steal Life, his gazed supply, or Death endow?
To pause in coffin-flesh or end the scene?
That is the private torment: Know thy fate
when Kismet, hem high, qualifies the muse,
but know so bare the braided whole, His feared Law,
until fate's verge, a red or tawny dawn
(both fade), is granted to the heart that fumed.
Endure or rot? My choice — whose tune-fond verbs
return the azure soul's repellent will —
reveals a howl-bruised heart, the meek as sane....

The rotten know a fly-hot snow of teeth;
clocks swerve the coals, and so I am confused:
Do I unleash into the now, thus feature?
Depart with haste; choke life, its gothic soul?
Do I Zen-path and grant for me time present?
Draw weary curtains, shattering their hurt?
Of acts (they mount)? Of noose? A wooden nail?
His infinite horizon or thy hem? Appeal!
Remember: man sees blindly.

POOR YORICK

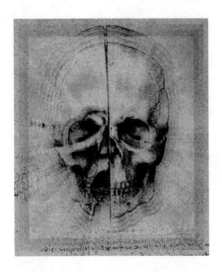

Dissections (or, The Pen and the Scalpel)

AELINDROME IN THE PLASTIC NUMBER
13247179572447460259

Tear the pen,
to pen
this yet-seen draw
words cut across.

It weaves
in letters
it escapes,
fathoms,
and, thus,
reforms —
and hopes fate
scatters it in leaves.

We cross
its cut and raw words,
yet see it open
the pent heart....

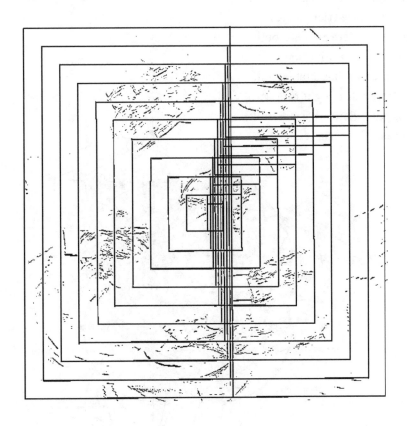

The Astrolabe

THE ASTROLABE TRIANGULATES

Log sure: Beneath a star atilt,
the astrolabe triangulates.
So, target here an atlas, built,
log sure, beneath a star atilt.
True reason has a tablet gilt,
a stable rule a night rotates....
Log sure! Beneath a star, atilt,
the astrolabe triangulates....

FURTHER ROTATIONS OF THE ASTROLABE

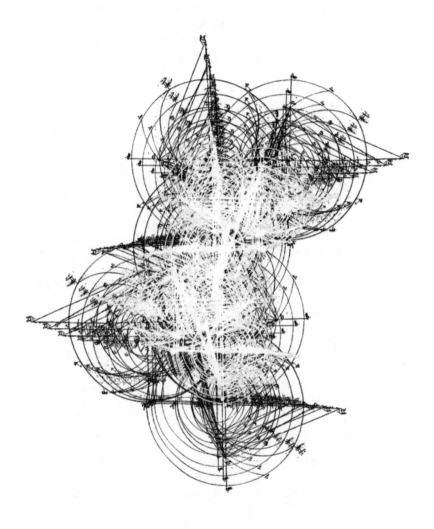

The Candle

Tile,
bottle,
mix —
u wull
I w&er.
*

If I
spill a poem,
it's a sun,
it's a c&le
we jewel
& cast, in us,
as time.
*

Opal lips
I fire,
& will a wax
I melt, to be lit.

WAXWORK PIXELS

poetic wax
billows beatific
ellipses,
to melt
in its pixels & jail.
time & flame
illuminate.
aurorae sweat & swell.
spilt, i wait & wail.

Sundials

THE HORIZONTAL DIAL

Laid,
an onus set,
a gnomon gates sun, on a dial....
> Sky rhythms fly by, wryly,
> by my crypt —
> by syzygy.
> Sulphur sun succumbs:
> Dusk dulls us, murmurs,
> blunts us up.

> Soft glows of hollow moon
> grow gnomon forms on
> ponds of rock.
> This night is finishing.
> Its vigil lifting, nitid shifting
> gilts this dish with twilit stirrings.

Restless edges represent.
(The steeple's lengths lessen
when the flexed degrees descend.)
> A raw and rampant
> dawn attracts a waltz
> and marks a path.
> Laid,
> an onus set,
> a gnomon gates sun, on a dial.

THE VERTICAL DIAL

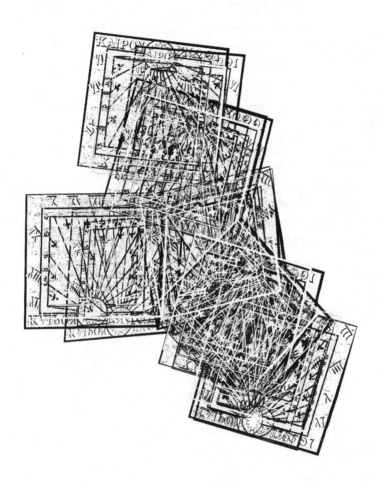

The String Section

> The string section:
> Intersecting host.
> The resting tonic's
> sonic tether — sting
> into secret things....

Noise: Lyre.
Venom: music.
I'm any drone, risen or of speed.
Divas send, as stress, a mood for a bass.
I host it.

> Cello, craft solos!
> Outrival a virtuoso!
> > Lost far, collect it. So, hiss....
> > > A bar of doom asserts sadness —
> > > avid deeps, for one siren or dynamic.
> > > I summon every lesion....

STRING QUARTET

Seismography

VOLCANO

A vale,
sirenic;

ito alpo
a red net's atlas;

a bared,
nude summit,
pure.

Pools loop,
erupt.

I'm mused....

Under
a basalt
as tender
as plasticine,
rise, lava.

SEISMOGRAPH

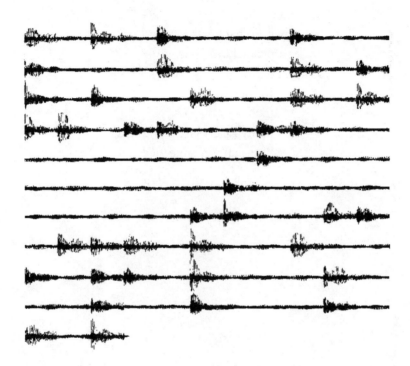

Enigma (for Alan Turing)

        Decode:
        Men awe, at that heathen spindle,
        to see any machine's ode.
        Cater, Enigma:
            I generate codes,
            inch —
            many ease, to lend pins heat;
            heat that we name, decode....

DECRYPT

```
QZKME PQYEI UGJGB ZMSUL MSIPM
QMCIL TNQIE ZWQOT OOITR FUVZL
XKPSN WFYWH GZXEN JYUHQ OQCPN
UUATG TFPBN VINXI SLWAV FQLUP
IWWKV OOZHB MHCUF LINNU EN
=============================
DECOD EMENA WEATT HATHE ATHEN
SPIND LETOS EEANY MACHI NESOD
ECATE RENIG MAIGE NERAT ECODE
SINCH MANYE ASETO LENDP INSHE
ATHEA TTHAT WENAM EDECO DE
```

121

The Feynman Diagram

UNIVOCALIC SONNET FOR THE ONE-ELECTRON
UNIVERSE OF FEYNMAN AND WHEELER

Elected speck: relentless, endless sphere —
engender, breed ensemble, hence effect;
reverse resettlement, cement the here;
re-enter, reel the verse; renew, reflect....
Re-represented seed! The presence swells.
Let essence be serene, emergent germ!
Strewn, never feel depleted, ever dwell.
The needle sews the text, the length, the term.
When schemes extend extremes (reversed, else free),
renewed events meet tethered, nestled nerves;
the skewered self emerges, per decree —
between the present newness, elder swerves....
       These self-elected scenes exceeded tense,
        when Wheeler's jest expressed the tenet hence.

CROSS-SECTION OF THE ONE-ELECTRON UNIVERSE

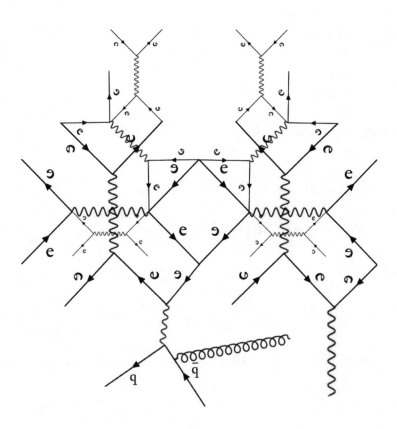

Chaos Theory

AELINDROME IN FEIGENBAUM'S FIRST CONSTANT
46692016091029906718

Sonatas perish, losing,
so fool thorn and nail.

Timeworn, find that surge
of tenfold change and haste.

Rearrange and hold.
Charge often.

Find that sun frail,
time worn,
and nothing so foolish, lost as persona.

FRACTAL SYMMETRIES

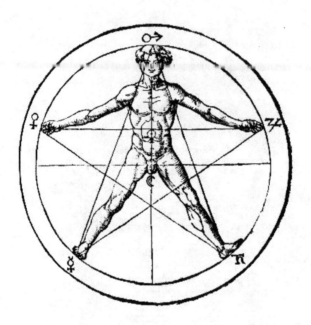

LABORATORY

Stray Arts (and Other Inventions) is a work of experimental formal poetry, with a focus both on traditional poetic forms and on more intricate literary constraints, such as anagrams, palindromes, and their variants. The book discusses a range of historically significant inventions, ideas, and discoveries, from multiple fields of human creativity.

Each of the textual poems explores its own balance between tradi tional poetic virtues and a premeditated alphabetical or lexical constraint. Some of the poems study special or simplified cases of existing forms; some create their own constraint; while others are structural indulgences—tests of technical complexity, whose poetry lies as much in the grandeur of their architecture as in the content of their words.

Similar to this last type are the visual poems scattered throughout the collection, which likewise assert that a poem's form isn't merely there to buttress its textual content—and is itself a poetic work.

The Reaping

THE TEXTUAL POEMS
Preceded by a simple Petrarchan sonnet in iambic monometer, "The Harvest" reflects on the history of agriculture, thereby making use of a common metaphor for the cycle of life and death. Each stanza features lines that are perfect anagrams of each other—the letters of each section thus reshuffling like tilled soil.

CHAOS AND THE FURROWS
In this visual poem, random paint splatters meet uniform digital lines, mimicking the chaos of sown seedlings among the order of man-made furrows.

Atoms, Gods, and the Void

THE TEXTUAL POEMS
The textual poems in this section are either letter-unit palindromes or composed of anagrammed lines. Adopting Democritus's favourite analogy for atomistic creation, the poems permute their letters, like particles, in order to atomise and revise classical myths. As an exercise in reinterpretation and metamorphosis, special attention is paid to the Romans' appropriation of Greek mythological figures—as well as to contemporaneous and later astronomical uses of Greco-Roman nomenclature, and to the more current, reimagined atomism of modern science.

PROMETHEUS AND HIS CREATION
This piece makes palindromic visual poetry—a mandala for mankind's creator—of a detail from *Prometheus Forms Man and Animates Him with Fire from Heaven* by Hendrik Goltzius (from the 1589 edition of Ovid's *Metamorphoses*).

Sacred Numbers

The aelindrome is a new constraint, which I devised during the autumn of 2012, after discovering the possibility and potential of "palindromes-by-pairs" ("Intense? I am Einstein!"). Aelindromes (derived from my initials: A. E.-lindromes) are a variation on traditional palindromes—however, instead of mirroring a repeated, fixed letter-unit, they reverse units of variable sizes, as determined by premeditated numerical sequences. That is, while palindromes-by-letter and palindromes-by-pairs use consistent, *homogeneous* units (1 and 2, respectively), aelindromes employ *heterogeneous* units, variously grouped according to underlying numerical palindromes.

An example: the phrase "Melody, a bloody elm" is an aelindrome structured by the numerical palindrome 1234321, since $[m]_1$ $[el]_2$ $[ody]_3$ $[a blo]_4$ reflects backward as $[a blo]_4$ $[ody]_3$ $[el]_2$ $[m]_1$. By convention, aelindromes are said to be "in" the forward incarnation of their sequence (up to and including its pivot). Thus, "Melody, a bloody elm" is an "aelindrome in 1234."

Note that, when parsing letters this way, a unit of zero letters will return as a unit of zero letters—absence reflects as absence. Thus, an aelindrome in 1234 has a structure identical to that of an aelindrome in, for example, 10020300000004.

By my technical definition of the aelindrome, word-unit palindromes that obey premeditated letter numbers—e.g., "I am mad, am I?" [12321]—while superficially aelindromic, cannot rightly be considered aelindromes. A palindrome cannot simultaneously adhere to homogeneous and heterogeneous units of palindromy. Put another way, the word-unit palindromism of such palindromes *overrules* any claim to aelindromism: Just as it would be absurd to call palindromes-by-letter "aelindromes in 111 (etc.)" or palindromes-by-pairs "aelindromes in 222 (etc.)," a word-unit palindrome that is patterned after premeditated letter numbers is merely a special case of palindrome-by-word (it is a palindrome-by-word that follows an additional letter-count restriction).

Aelindromes, then, cannot be palindromes. They exhibit palindromic bidirectionality in the numerical sequences underpinning them, but *never even the possibility* of bidirectionality in a consistent linguistic unit (letter, word, line, sentence, paragraph, etc.). Aelindromes have palindromic bones, but not palindromic skin. By this fact, there can be no "word-unit aelindromes" at all, since it is always possible for grouped words to be coherently redistributed into lines—thus making any apparent word-unit aelindrome merely a restitched line-unit palindrome (with specified, reflected word counts for each line, as in symmetrical pattern poetry). Similar applies to lines and to stanzas; it follows that, as a textual exercise, aelindromes are an inherently and unambiguously letter-based constraint.

The aelindromes featured in "Sacred Numbers" are structured by numerical palindromes derived from the decimal expansions of, respectively, the golden ratio (φ), the square root of two ($\sqrt{2}$), Euler's number (e), pi (π), and the fraction 2357/9999 (which repeats the single-digit prime numbers). Each aelindrome is aelindromic in as many figures as expressed beneath its title. A breakdown of one of the pi aelindromes is below.

The Sector
314159

[Spi]$_3$[r]$_1$[al te]$_4$[a]$_1$[rs are]$_5$
[cut.
A secto]$_9$[r's are]$_5$[a]$_1$[alte]$_4$[r]$_1$[s:
Pi.]$_3$

VISUAL AELINDROME IN e

This piece presents a form derived from angular permutations determined by the decimal expansion of e. Making use of all five of the sequences employed in the preceding textual poems, this visual poem's construction began with a sketch from Heinrich Cornelius Agrippa's *Libri tres de occulta philosophia* (the sketch preceding this "Laboratory"). In the original sketch, Agrippa illustrates man upon a cross whose arms are of equal length (which represents √2), a pentagram (representing φ), and a circle (representing π). Here, Agrippa's image was repeated, side-by-side, to create a row of 7 (the largest single-digit prime). This row was then positioned at 2 degrees from the horizontal (since the first digit of e is 2), before being replicated at 9 degrees (i.e., a further 7 degrees up, since e's second digit is 7), and so on, until the 90-degree point was crossed (which occurred when the expansion had reached its twentieth digit, making this poem an aelindrome in 27182818284590452353). Following this, the sequence was reversed (35325409548281828172), and each digit in turn was added to the angle. On an aesthetic whim, the result was then reproduced in white, at 2/3 size, and pasted over the larger structure. The entire work was then, in a statement of pure symmetry, reflected vertically. As with linguistic aelindromes, however, there is no left-right (or "narrative") symmetry in the final image itself, but rather a symmetry hidden in the sequence that underpins it.

The Lilith Sonnets

In a nod to the historical relationship between occultism and the practices of cryptology and symbology, "The Lilith Sonnets" explores themes of witchcraft and paganism through a series of constrained and visual poems. Each of the suite's sonnets obeys a different alphabetical constraint: "Lilith and Hecate" is composed of fourteen perfectly anagrammed lines; "Lilith and Pan" is palindromic by letter; "Lilith and Ra" is palindromic by pairs of letters; and "Lilith and Hades" is a palindrome-by-word. While the first four sonnets are pentametric, and Shakespearean in rhyme scheme, the fifth, a pangram (using every letter of the alphabet at least once), is dimetric and Spenserian. Accompanying the sonnets are two visual poems that play with the visual poetry of paganic symbols.

Weapons of War

ARROWS AND BOWS

"Arrows and Bows" uses palindromic and visual poetry to depict imaginary scenes of archery in medieval warfare. The first palindrome is a palindrome-by-letter and the second a palindrome-by-pairs. The third is palindromic by blocks of three letters (that is, "by-triples") and the fourth by blocks of four ("by-quartets"). Each palindrome is complemented by a glyphic visual work, illustrative of the palindrome's contents.

WARS OF ÞE ROSES AND ÞORNS

"Fog of War" is a bilingual palindrome whose first stanza is in English and whose second is in Welsh. "Niwl o Rhyfel" sees each stanza translated. This union of English and Welsh is followed by a statement on Richard III's death at the Battle of Bosworth Field (a battle won by Henry Tudor, making Tudor the only Welshman ever to claim the English throne). Here, it is revealed that the fatal blow to Richard III was most likely dealt by a popular fifteenth-century dagger sharing its name with a poetic form: the rondel. Accordingly, "Palindrome-Rondel for Richard þe Þird" is a palindromic rondel composed of iambic alexandrines. Moreover, in this rondel, the Old English letter þ ("thorn") has been resurrected for the dual purposes of increased palindromic vocabulary and medieval affectation. This archaic letter is then similarly used as the basis for two shorter poems: Firstly, a tautogrammatic octave, written in iambic tetrameter and loosely describing the events that took place during the Battle of Bosworth Field; and secondly, a poem of anagrammed lines, obeying the medieval Welsh form "Englyn Penfyr" (a three-line poem, syllable count 10-7-7, whose second and third end-rhymes match the penultimate syllable of the first line, and whose first line's end-rhyme returns as the fourth syllable of line two).

THE BODIES BELOW US
"The Bodies Below Us" is a symmetrical visual poem made from Plate 214 of the *Codex Wallerstein* (1400s). The original image depicts a half-sword being thrust against a mordhau, in longsword combat. Both combatants are equipped with rondel daggers.

Five Romantics (in Firm Octaves)

THE TEXTUAL POEMS
"Idyll" comprises two ottave rime, one palindromic by letter and the other palindromic by pairs of letters. Each is written in iambic tetrameter and in a style paying homage to the Romantic Poets. It is followed by a sequence of five iambic triolets, written for five poets, in which each poem repeatedly anagrams a line from one of its subject's most famous poems. These are: "The nightmare Life-In-Death was she," (Coleridge, "The Rime of the Ancient Mariner," 1798); "I wandered lonely as a cloud" (Wordsworth, "I Wandered Lonely as a Cloud," 1807); "She walks in beauty, like the night" (Byron, "She Walks in Beauty," 1813); "'My name is Ozymandias, king of kings:" (Shelley, "Ozymandias," 1818); and "Fled is that music:—do I wake or sleep?" (Keats, "Ode to a Nightingale," 1819).

The section ends with a juvenile collage dedicated to two Romantic Poets, and featuring a typed, printed, and glued palindromic poem in their honour. Also included are three pressed daffodils, contemporaneous sketches of the poets, drafts of "I Wandered Lonely as a Cloud" and "Kubla Khan," a detail from "A Field of Yellow Flowers" by Vincent van Gogh, and an illustration, by Gustave Doré, for "The Rime of the Ancient Mariner."

Prometheus Bound

THE TEXTUAL POEMS
The "Sonnets for Frankenstein" are Shakespearean in rhyme scheme and composed in iambic pentameter; the first is palindromic by letter, while the second has perfectly anagrammed lines. The poems discuss the events of Mary Shelley's novel.

Written for Herman Melville's *Moby-Dick*, "The White Whale" obeys a stricter combinatorial restriction: The first of the poems is a palindrome-by-letter, while the second is a palindrome-by-pairs. These two palindromes are perfect anagrams of each other.

Conflating the novels to which it refers, "Prometheus and the Creature" studies *Frankenstein* and *Moby-Dick* as congruent tales of Promethean tragedy. The poem is in four terza rima tercets, all perfect anagrams of each other.

THE RIGGING
Completing the suite, "The Rigging" features an abstract representation of the rigging typical of nineteenth-century whaling ships (many of which would later be repurposed for Arctic expeditions, such as Walton's in *Frankenstein*). Below this shipless rigging is a tangle of lines, mimicking the ropes' reflection in water.

Observatory

THE TEXTUAL POEMS

"Observatory" begins with two constrained triads: "Orion" and "Boötes Void." Each triad features a poem of anagrammed lines, a palindrome-poem, and a perfect anagram of this palindrome. Next are "Remote Meteor"—a Petrarchan, monometer sonnet—and "Venus", a pangrammatic Shakespearean sonnet, in iambic dimeter, which uses every letter of the alphabet at least once. "Selene" and "Earth" resurrect the tripartite structure used for "Orion" and "Boötes Void"; in the case of "Earth," the palindrome is a palindrome-by-pairs.

GALILEAN MOONS

Prefaced by an anagram-poem of the style featured throughout this suite, the final piece makes visual poetry from sketches by Galileo Galilei—specifically, Galileo's earliest drawings of the largest moons of Jupiter. (The sketches are believed to have been made during or shortly after the moons' discovery.)

The Piano

ROSE IDOL

"Rose Idol" presents a short palindrome, accompanied by three images of a piano, each in a different shade: greyscale red, black, and white. The piano depicted is a 1726 "Cristofori" piano (Bartolomeo Cristofori di Francesco is generally considered the inventor of the piano). The original sketch, taken from *Encyclopædia Britannica*, 11th ed., Vol. 21, p. 565, has been, in each case, recoloured and set against the decimal expansion of the twelfth root of two, as retyped on a restored antique typewriter.

RED PIANO

"Red Piano" is a Shakespearean sonnet, in iambic pentameter, and an aelindrome in the twelfth root of 2 (which is the ratio of the frequencies of any two adjacent piano keys—that is, in any octave, the frequency of A multiplied by $^{12}\sqrt{2}$ gives the frequency of A#, and the

136

frequency of A# multiplied by $^{12}\sqrt{2}$ gives the frequency of B, etc.). This aelindrome is taken to 47 significant figures (as detailed in its title).

BLACK PIANO

"Black Piano" is a musical aelindrome that groups beats, rather than letters, according to the decimal expansion of $^{12}\sqrt{2}$. The piece is intended for unaccompanied piano.

WHITE PIANO

"White Piano" is a visual aelindrome in the decimal expansion of $^{12}\sqrt{2}$, composed according to the same angular method as that employed for "Visual Aelindrome in e." This visual poem uses as its source image the opening two bars of Alexander Scriabin's Piano Sonata no. 7 —also known as "White Mass."

The Eureka Sonnets

"The Eureka Sonnets" studies six revolutionary thinkers from the worlds of literature and science: Edgar Allan Poe, Charles Darwin, Niels Bohr, Albert Einstein, Marie Curie, and Jorge Luis Borges. All six poems are Shakespearean sonnets, in iambic pentameter; two of the sonnets are palindromes-by-letter, while the others employ anagrammed lines. The suite concludes with "Eureka," a monometer Petrarchan sonnet, complemented by visual poetry made from Charles Darwin's most famous journal entry.

Passion and Permutation

THE TEXTUAL POEMS
"Passion and Permutation" begins with a simple anagram-poem: two six-line stanzas whose lines are perfect anagrams of the word "permutations." This is followed by a series of meditations on two of art's greatest inventors—Arnaut Daniel, who created the sestina poetic form, and Pablo Picasso, arguably the most prolific and celebrated visual artist of the twentieth century.

The premise of this section is that in every work of art (and in every artist) there exists a unique negotiation between a calculating, structural idealism and a more explosive, expressive obsession. For Jorge Luis Borges, this complementarity was that of "algebra and fire." For Italo Calvino, it was "crystal and flame." In this suite of poems, the lives and works of Arnaut Daniel and Pablo Picasso are examined through the crystal lens of "permutation" and the flames of "lustful passion."

Both Daniel and Picasso wed their creative ardour to a more detached structural aesthetic: Daniel composed his poetry according to the cyclical interlocking of end words. Picasso portrayed his muses through the distanced, chrono-geometric permutability of cubist multiperspectivism.

Accordingly, the poems of "Daniel and Picasso" discuss passion while using structures that emphasise transformation within repetition. "Divine Comedy" finds Arnaut Daniel where Dante left him: suffering a cyclical penance in Purgatory for his many lustful sins. The poem comprises six lines of anapaestic tetrameter, each featuring exactly six six-letter words. "Ardour Tiding" sees Picasso's art as a beach, recurrently transformed by tides of passionate creativity—reappearing the same, but changed. The poem is a palindrome-by-pairs whose shape traces the path of a shifting tide.

Next is "Anagram-Sestina for Pablo Picasso," which presents a critical analysis of Picasso's oeuvre, all the while cycling end-words and permuting a fixed set of 36 letters. The poem is written in iambic pentameter, and its envoi employs the traditional word orders: 2-5, 4-3, and 6-1.

The final textual poem is both a sestina and a palindrome-by-letter. It follows Arnaut Daniel, wandering lost and recanting his lust, amidst fiery purgatorial mists—all the while singing about and within the cyclical form he invented. Rather than fighting them, the poem embraces the onerous trappings of its combinatorial constraint, to affect the confusion, the repetitiveness, and the overall tedious, emotionless *drabness* of the once-passionate bard's purgatorial state. As with the preceding sestina, all lines are in iambic pentameter, and the envoi obeys the word orders 2-5, 4-3, and 6-1.

VISUAL SESTINA
The section concludes with a simple visual poem, in which glyphic Arnaut Daniels are permuted according to the pattern of the form he devised.

Mirror, Image

"Mirror, Image" features two iambic Shakespearean sonnets, each of which tangentially discusses, divided between its octave and its sestet, an optical instrument and a phenomenon involving reflection. The first sonnet, which addresses the camera obscura (octave) and the infinity mirror (sestet), is palindromic by letter. The second sonnet, whose subjects are the reflecting telescope (octave) and reflections in water (sestet), is palindromic by word. The two sonnets are perfect anagrams of each other.

As a complement to these anagrammed palindrome-sonnets, "The Shattered Mirror" presents an even more extreme experiment in palindrome-anagram combinatorial restriction: In this piece, the four subjects discussed in the preceding sonnets are re-examined within short, riddle-like palindromes of various styles: The camera obscura (top left) appears in a palindrome-by-letter; the infinity mirror (bottom left) in a palindrome-by-word. The reflecting telescope (top right) is addressed in a palindrome-by-pairs-of-words, while reflections in water (bottom right) are discussed within a palindrome-by-pairs-of-letters. All four palindromes are perfect anagrams of each other. Moreover, each of these palindromes is a perfect anagram of the introductory paragraph (at the top of page 98).

OPTICKS

"Opticks" is a digital visual poem that uses modelling software to map figures from *Cyclopaedia: or, An Universal Dictionary of Arts and Sciences* (Ephraim Chambers, 1728) onto human eyeballs.

Museum

"Museum" begins with two sonnets in iambic dimeter. The first has lines that are all perfect anagrams of its title; it discusses the legend of Atlantis. The second is a palindrome-by-letter, composed for the "Great Hymn to the Aten" (a poem-hymn written in fourteenth-century BC Egypt, for the sun-disk deity Aten, and traditionally attributed to the New Kingdom pharaoh Akhenaten). Each sonnet is joined by an ancient text that has been cropped, discoloured, desaturated and sharpened: "Atlantis Wished" features a distorted portion of the Gilgamesh cuneiform tablet on which the Great Flood myth is recorded. "Great Hymn to the Aten" features a rendering of Akhenaten's hymn (adapted from a drawing of the original, via N. de G. Davies, *The Rock Tombs of El Amarna*, part VI, "The Egypt Exploration Fund" (London, 1908)).

THE PRINTING PRESS
This poem-pair places a palindrome alongside concrete poetry made from desaturated text abstracted from the *Gutenberg Bible* (the first major book to be printed in Europe using mass-produced movable metal type).

THE SOLILOQUY
"Halt Me" is a line-for-line perfect anagram of Hamlet's "To Be or Not to Be" soliloquy, as it appears in the *First Folio* (1623). The anagram takes direct inspiration from its source material's theme and poetic metre. (Note: all instances of ſ have been converted to s.) "Poor Yorick" is a distortion of a skull diagram by Leonardo da Vinci.

DISSECTIONS (OR, THE PEN AND THE SCALPEL)
"Dissections" presents an aelindrome in the decimal expansion of the plastic number (ρ). Accompanying this aelindrome is a visual poem depicting the repeated, rescaled "dissection" of a soft plastic surface, by a scalpel. The surface has been dissected according to aspect ratios of ρ^2 (which famously divides a square into three mutually non-congruent, similar rectangles).

THE ASTROLABE

In this piece, a triolet whose lines are perfect anagrams of each other is placed alongside visual poetry made from a diagram from the book *Compositio et operatio astrolabii* (a twelfth-century volume on the construction and operation of astrolabes).

THE CANDLE

"The Candle" features a palindrome that uses ampersands in place of the trigraph "and." This palindrome is then anagrammed, with the resulting anagram presented in an all-lowercase font created specifically for this book.

SUNDIALS

The eight stanzas of "The Horizontal Dial" describe the confused shadows that form on a horizontal sundial, between dusk and dawn and through moonlight. The first stanza, also the last, is a palindrome-by-letter. The central six stanzas are univocalic lipograms, whose single vowels appear in reverse alphabetical order: y, u, o, i, e, a. Complementing this horizontal sundial is a visual poem made from a desaturated and sharpened photograph of the vertical sundial at Ely Cathedral, Cambridgeshire.

THE STRING SECTION

Here, a palindrome and anagram-poem "duet" meets a visual "String Quartet" made from Mozart's stave notation for "String Quartet No. 13 in D minor, K.173" and images sourced from *The Syntagma Musicum* by Michael Praetorius (1620).

SEISMOGRAPHY

"Seismography" begins with "Volcano," a palindrome-by-letter. To create "Seismograph," seismogram-like waveforms were generated by performing this palindrome on an acoustic guitar—with the letters a to g played as their corresponding notes and the letters h to z left as pauses.

ENIGMA (FOR ALAN TURING)

Using the methods of its titular machine, "Enigma" generates a con-
crete poem from a palindrome-by-pairs, offering the latter as the
"solution" to an encrypted text. Enigma machines encrypted
messages through polyalphabetic encipherments: certain models, like
the one replicated here, used a triadic encipherment, performed by a
spindle with three rotors. Each rotor would be set to a specific starting
position (a letter of the alphabet), the first of which provided a simple
substitution cipher. A series of electrical plate contacts and pins
would then communicate the message along the spindle, through the
turning rotors, thus enciphering each letter two more times. To gen-
erate this poem's encrypted text (QZKME, etc.), and in tribute to Alan
Turing, whose wartime efforts helped crack the Enigma code, the
three rotors' starting positions have here been set to Turing's initials:
A, M, and T.

THE FEYNMAN DIAGRAM

"The Feynman Diagram" presents a diptych whose subject is
Feynman and Wheeler's "One-Electron Universe" hypothesis.
According to the hypothesis, the reason that all electrons possess
exactly the same charge and mass is that there is, in fact, only one
electron in the universe, which has created its manifold incarnations
by travelling both backwards and forwards in time—its backwards
appearances being as positrons. While the hypothesis was mostly
meant in jest, in Feynman diagrams there is no clear distinction
between electrons and backwards-travelling positrons. In honour of
the purity and absurdity of this idea, "The Feynman Diagram"
features both a Shakespearean sonnet, univocalic in e, and an
improvised Feynman diagram depicting a "cross-section" of the
one-electron universe (complete with a quark-antiquark pair, mate-
rialising from electron-positron annihilation—a hint, perhaps, that
all matter arises from this single, almighty electron).

CHAOS THEORY

"Chaos Theory" begins with an aelindrome in the decimal expansion of Feigenbaum's First Constant (which describes the rate at which dynamical period-doubling bifurcation, and thus full chaotic behaviour, occurs). Although primarily inspired by mathematical and physical manifestations of chaotic behaviour, the poem also alludes to analogous theories of chaos in the fields of music and psychology. This textual poem is complemented by "Fractal Symmetries," which makes symmetrical visual poetry from a simple, command-line depiction of the Mandelbrot set (the source image is a reproduction of the first ever recorded image of the Mandelbrot set—it has been taken from Wikipedia, where it is attributed to Elphaba).

Praise for *Stray Arts (and Other Inventions)*

"I've seen people able to do perfect bottom deals at casino poker tables for 100 thousand dollar stakes, under heat. I've seen people able to do bottom deals at illegal mob games where everyone was carrying. This poetry is only a bit safer but way, way harder. And impresses me more. I love it."
—Penn Jillette

"Anthony Etherin renders all my own virtuoso ventures obsolete. I truly covet this book."
—Christian Bök

"Anthony Etherin is a hard taskmaster with language, making it jump through hoops, run long distances backwards, and then turn in on itself, in a strenuous series of contortions that leave it gleaming with word-sweat — but all this exercise is more than worth it, because the poems Anthony produces are dictionaries of possibilities, maps of linguistic futures that are well worth exploring if you want to find joy and delight and jaw-dropping skill."
—Ian McMillan

Most of the poems in this collection have previously appeared else-
where, either on Twitter or in the following pamphlets, journals, and
anthologies:

PAMPHLETS FROM PENTERACT PRESS
"Ratio," "Matrix," and "Geometry" (as *Aelindromes* φ- π-√2, 2017)
"Prime Aelindromes" (2019)
"Palindrome Rondel for Richard þe Þird"
        (as *Wars of þe Roses and Þorns*, 2016)
"Palindrome-Sestina for Arnaut Daniel" (2017)
"The Frankenstein Sonnets" (in *Poems for Frankenstein*, 2019)
"The White Whale" (2017)
"Red Piano" (2018)
"Mirror, Image" (without "Opticks", 2017)
"Atlantis Wished" and "Great Hymn to the Aten"
        (as a leaflet pair, 2018)

PAMPHLETS FROM ELSEWHERE
"Lilith and Hecate," "Lilith and Pan,"
"Lilith and Ra," and "Lilith and Hades"
        (as *The Lilith Sonnets*, No Press, 2018)
"Arrows and Bows" (Timglaset Editions, 2017)
"Anagram-Sestina for Pablo Picasso" (No Press, 2018)
"Five Romantics (in Firm Octaves)" [without "Idyll"]
        (No Press, 2017)
"Anagram-Sonnet for Jorge Luis Borges" (No Press, 2016)
"Selene" [parts two and three only] (Spacecraft Press, 2018)
"Halt Me" (Spacecraft Press, 2019)

PRINT JOURNALS AND ANTHOLOGIES

"Permutations" (*Concrete & Constraint*, Penteract Press, 2018)

"Famine Moon" (*Reflections*, Penteract Press, 2019)

"Palindrome-Sonnet" from "The Frankenstein Sonnets"
        (*Reflections*, Penteract Press, 2019)

"Anagram-Sonnet" from "The Frankenstein Sonnets"
        [early version] (*Touch the Donkey no.16*, 2018)

"The White Whale" (*Reflections*, Penteract Press, 2019)

"Eureka" (*ToCall no.3*, 2019)

"The Printing Press" (*ToCall no.1*, 2018)

"Volcano" (*Reflections*, Penteract Press, 2019)

"The Feynman Diagram"
        (*Concrete & Constraint*, Penteract Press, 2018)

ONLINE JOURNALS

"Iliad and Aeneid" (*Five2One Magazine*, 2016)

"Asymptote" (*Cordite Poetry Review*, 2017)

"Geometry" (*The Account Magazine*, 2016)

"For Wordsworth" (*The Wordsworth Trust*, 2016)

"Palindrome-Sonnet" from "The Frankenstein Sonnets"
        [early version] (*Eunoia Review*, 2017)

"Aelindrome in the Decimal Expansion of the Plastic Number"
        (*Burning House Press*, 2018)

"The Astrolabe" (*talking about strawberries all of the time*, 2018)

"The Horizontal Dial" (*Dusie*, 2018)

"Enigma (for Alan Turing)" (*Burning House Press*, 2019)

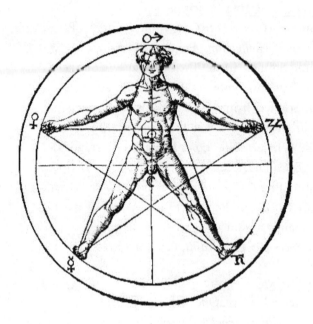

THE UTU
SONNETS

ANTHONY ETHERIN

The Utu Sonnets

OSIRIS BLED   9

UTU'S RAIN   11

ENLIL'S IMAGES   13

BELOW IS BELOW   15

THE END ISN'T ONLY THE END   17

LOST SOL   19

REST, LUNA LUSTRE   21

NOTES   23

Utu, sun rubs us.
Dusk cuts.
Dumb mud, stuck, suds us.
Burn us, Utu....

The Players
(by Tradition and in Order of Appearance)

<u>SUMERIAN</u>

Utu, God of the Sun
Inanna, Goddess of Love, Beauty and War
Ninurta, God of Agriculture and Healing
An, Supreme God and God of the Sky
Enki, God of the Waters
Enlil, God of the Air
Ereshkigal, Goddess of the Underworld
Ninsun, Goddess and Mother of Gilgamesh
Ki, Goddess of the Earth

<u>EGYPTIAN</u>

Osiris, God of the Afterlife
Nut, Goddess of the Sky
Aten, God of the Sun (Sun Disc)
Anubis, God of the Underworld
Amun, God of the Air
Ra, God of the Sun
Nu, God of the Primordial Waters
Set, God of Deserts and Disorder

GREEK

Athena, Goddess of Wisdom and War

Siren, Mythological Monster(s)

Muses, Goddesses of Literature, Science, and Art

Ares, God of War

Eros, God of Love and Sex

Orion, Mythological Huntsman

Apollo, God of Poetry and the Sun

Dionysus, God of Wine and Festivity

Aphrodite, Goddess of Love and Beauty

Atalanta, Mythological Huntress

Poseidon, God of the Seas

Eris, Goddess of Strife and Discord

Atlas, God (Titan) of the Sky

Hera, Goddess of Women and Marriage

Artemis, Goddess of the Hunt and the Moon

Gaia, Goddess (Titaness) of the Earth

Pan, God of the Wild

ROMAN

Venus, Goddess of Love and Beauty
Diana, Goddess of the Hunt and the Moon
Luna, Goddess of the Moon
Juno, Goddess of the State
Mars, God of War
Sol, God of the Sun
Saturn, God of Generation
Remus, Mythological Twin
Neptune, God of the Seas

Osiris Bled

Our Sun! **Athena** trembled **Utu**'s flame.
Olympus wed a temple, wept a sea.
Osiris bled beneath the spiral tree
of **Venus**, where **Inanna** carved her name.

Ordained inside a **Siren** skull I claim,
ornate **Ninurta**'s wings deter ennui.
Outside a glassy gateway, less a key,
on Eden is a sun and inner blame.

O, pagan **Muses** stir us and install
old arias **Diana** did retain —
one epithet, in **Luna**'s lantern, tall.
(On **Utu**'s altar, **An** saw **Ares** slain.)

O, astral island! **Luna** adds us all.
Osiris jars us: dust in jaded rain.

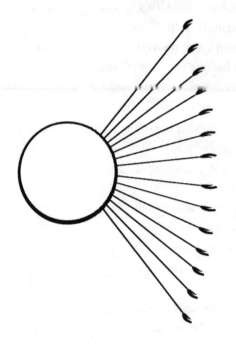

Utu's Rain

Near **Utu**'s rain sits able **Luna** blue —
amid **Nut**'s open rite, tall suns atop —
else **Eros** sins, else **Enki** ends anew;
lest **Juno** ruin dawn, lest **Aten** drop.

Upon July, akin, late **Mars** pens wars:
"Rain data — anti, anti, rain idea.
Undo duet. Defy main holy laws.
Rain arid sand. Nail Eden (Asia Near)."

Mars' omen dies, that aria then said.
Sigh: **Ares** ebbs, amid some Eden sand —
till **Luna** sees wars gain man's avid dead;
till suns turn east, draw over **Utu**'s land.

Lull ages. Echo area. Ring lyre.
Sol's **Aten**. **Utu**'s epic halo fire.

Enlil's Images

Arenas. **Enlil**'s images innate:
Athena. Sanded season. Plains' lament.
Orion's radial, Aegean strait.
Untidy saunas. Julian assent.

Inanna: Landed beauty. Warmth adored.
Arisen annals. Poetry divine!
Erotic, narrow shadow deeply poured.
Diana's battle. **Venus**'s design.

Anubis: Sunken wreath. United. Phased.
(Assign demise! Assess unjust ordeal!)
Osiris: Sacred mortal. Fallen. Raised.
Finale ritual. Burial unreal.

Apollo: Sunlit nature. Summer willed.
Athena: Wisest lustre. Autumn killed.

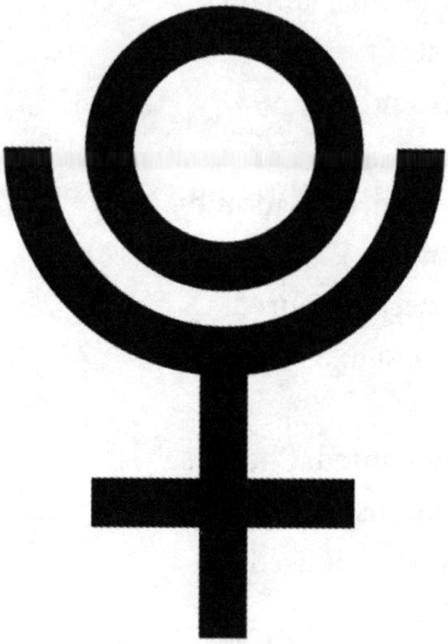

Below Is Below

Go ever, spirits, and land auras where —
below **Ereshkigal**, aside taboo —
demise led **Dionysus** to declare
infinity, in **Aphrodite** true.

Rise, **Saturn**'s annals, mid all manna, dust.
Plea **An**'s lament unseen — an inland war.
Sure **Luna** issues **Atalanta**, just.
Just **Atalanta** issues **Luna** sure.

War inland, an unseen lament **An**'s plea,
dust manna — all mid annals, **Saturn**'s rise...
True **Aphrodite**, in infinity,
declare, to **Dionysus**, led demise —

taboo aside, **Ereshkigal** below
(where auras land and spirits ever go).

The End Isn't Only the End

Osiris dies, eternally returns,
Amun's disguise illuminating **Nut**,
Inanna's tree, a flame **Athena** burns....
A law is read: Promethean pursuit.

Poseidon's sea a new **Ninurta**'s land,
Julys adore the dirt **Diana** scales.
Awaken dales to all, beloved sand!
Beloved sand, to all, awaken dales.

Diana scales the dirt Julys adore:
Ninurta's land. A new **Poseidon**'s sea.
Promethean pursuit is read a law —
Athena burns a flame, **Inanna**'s tree.

Illuminating **Nut**, **Amun**'s disguise
eternally returns. **Osiris** dies.

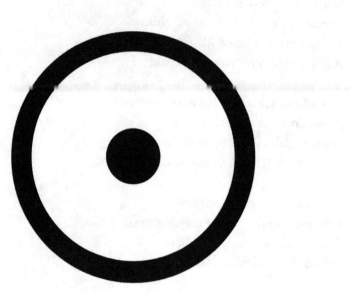

Lost Sol

No omen, I left **Sol**. Pure **Venus**, roar....
Noon sat, run ink (nil, as I met **Ra**'s deed).
Tense **Nut** pens **Remus**. **Utu** saps a war.
Nu, ray a bale. We jewel, at all, a creed.

Test light, **Ninsun**, in **Eris** — **Atlas** laid.
Nu, say a bad. A hill asserts I did
dim **An**, an idle **Hera**'s gods, an aid....
(**Diana**'s dogs are held in **An**, amid.)

Did I stress all I had? A bay, a sun....
Dial, salt a **Siren** in us. Ninth, gilt **Set**.
Deer call a tale. We jewel a bay, a run....
Raw asp! As **Utu**, Sumer's **Neptune**'s net.

Deeds **Artemis** a link: **Ninurta**'s noon.
Ra (or, Sun Ever Up). Lost, feline Moon.

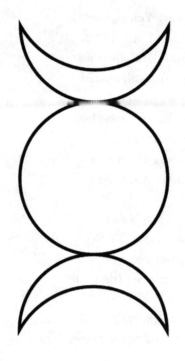

Rest, Luna Lustre

Athena! An inertia rolls a land.
Pen at her wounds a new ill: **Luna** lust.
Muse, poets yet dull fire we so demand:
Sand **Ki**. **An**'s cedar. Idly, **Juno**'s trust.

In **Gaia**, meet a sin I sub — a nest.
I ravel. I dare bait, so phrase, a sun.
A land, I unarm egos' endless rest.
In **Ra**, rain, stress lends ego, me, a run....

Diana, **Luna**'s seraph, so it bared.
Alive, **Ra** ties **Anubis** in a set.
Me — I, against, rust no July I dared.
Scan kind, sand made, so we refill duets....

Yet pose must **Luna**! Lull wines and our wheat.
End **Pan**, all solar. Tier **Inanna**. Heat.

The Utu Sonnets presents a sequence of seven rigidly constrained sonnets. The first sonnet obeys the Petrarchan scheme, while the remaining six obey the Shakespearean. All seven sonnets are in iambic pentameter.

"Atoms, Gods, and the Void," from my book *Stray Arts*, used palindromes and anagrams to rewrite scenes and characters from ancient mythologies—shuffling the atoms of these legends as the letters themselves were shuffled on the page. *The Utu Sonnets* takes this idea further, implementing an array of highly strict formal constraints to create a nonsensical, hallucinatory lore.

A total of 43 figures from Sumerian, Egyptian, Greek, and Roman mythologies appear in this sonnet sequence.

The first sonnet, "Osiris Bled," features only 14 instances of the letter o, with each o appearing at the beginning of a line.

The second sonnet, "Utu's Rain," uses only four-letter words—and the third sonnet, "Enlil's Images," only six-letter words.

The remaining four sonnets present various types of palindrome: "Below Is Below" is a palindrome by word. "The End Isn't Only the End" is palindromic by pairs of words. "Lost Sol" is a palindrome by letter. And "Rest, Luna Lustre" is palindromic by pairs of letters.

Moreover, all seven sonnets are perfect anagrams of each other.

Each sonnet is accompanied by a mythological symbol relating in some way to the text.

Acknowledgements

Thank you to Will Evans and the team at Deep Vellum for combining these books into a single edition—and for allowing me the freedom to present the books in their original formatting.

Many thanks also to Christian Bök for the wonderful foreword, and to Penn Jillette, Ian McMillan, Anthony Horowitz, and George Szirtes for their words of support throughout this project.

I am very grateful to everyone who has supported my poetry over the years, in particular my generous Patreon supporters and my enthusiastic followers on social media.

Most of all, thank you to Clara Etherin, to whom this book, and all my work, is dedicated.

Anthony Etherin is an experimental formalist poet and musician who specialises in working under strict procedural constraints. The inventor of several new literary restrictions, his poetry also combines traditional poetic forms with established alphabetical constraints, such as palindromes and anagrams. He frequently tweets poetry @Anthony_Etherin. He lives on the border of England and Wales.